GOD
MADE THE ANIMALS

Written by Dandi

Did you ever wonder
What God had in mind
When He made the birds
And beasts of every kind?

Cows and sheep and leopards –
All things, I do believe,
God created creatures
For Adam and for Eve.

Don't forget the journey
Made in Noah's ark!
Two by two they traveled
From zebra to aardvark.

When the flood was over,
Noah sent a dove.
In the sky a rainbow
Promised us God's love.

Lions God created
Roared in Daniels den.
Angels shut the lions' mouths.
David said, "Amen!"

God knew what was needed
For Jonah to prevail.
Just in time Ol' Jonah
Was swallowed by a whale.

Why did God make donkeys?
People needed them!
Mary rode a donkey
Up to Bethlehem.

Wise men rode on camels
The Christ Child to behold.
Camels brought them safely
To bring their gifts of gold.

Jesus told a story
About a lamb so lost:
"I would search and find it,
No matter what the cost."

Good thing God made fish
'Cause he met our needs again.
Jesus said, "Come follow,
And we will fish for men!"

God gave us such creatures –
No one should destroy!
Cats and dogs and parrots –
All pets to enjoy.

Take care of God's creatures,
Sent here from above.
Why did God make animals?
So YOU can give them love!

FOUR FAMOUS GREEK PLAYS

EDITED, WITH AN INTRODUCTION

BY

PROF. PAUL LANDIS, 1893- ed.

Play Anthology Reprint Series

BOOKS FOR LIBRARIES PRESS
FREEPORT, NEW YORK

PA
3626
. A2
L$_x$3
1971

First Published 1929
Reprinted 1971

INTERNATIONAL STANDARD BOOK NUMBER:
0-8369-8224-X

LIBRARY OF CONGRESS CATALOG CARD NUMBER:
77-173624

PRINTED IN THE UNITED STATES OF AMERICA
BY
NEW WORLD BOOK MANUFACTURING CO., INC.
HALLANDALE, FLORIDA 33009

CONTENTS

INTRODUCTION

THE Greek drama is the most convincing testimony we have to the fact that great literature is timeless and therefore always modern. Homer carries a still greater burden of years, and Sappho's songs have come to us in scarred and jagged fragments, like the remains of buried statues; but one was a simple story, directly told, of war and the beauty of women and the love of friends and family, and the other a passionate cry from a woman's heart. These are permanently moving things, and in Homer and Sappho there is little of the débris of bygone literary conventions to hide the treasure. The drama is different. It, too, tells stories of elemental human passions, but it must speak to us across twenty-five hundred years, not only in a language that for half that time has been a stranger to the lips of man, it must speak also through an art form more foreign to us than even its names and stories.

The dramatic is peculiar among literary forms in the strength of the conventions which it develops, conventions upon which the author leans for support and by which he is limited in the exercise of his genius. The dramatist, instead of speaking directly to his reader, must depend upon a group of actors to present his story to the audience, also in the group. Unless, therefore, he is writing a "closet-drama"—and the Greeks never did—the author must govern himself always by the circumstances surrounding the performance of his piece. Chief among these are the occasion when the play is to be performed and the architectural characteristics of the theatre. A proper appreciation of Shakespeare demands some knowledge of the Elizabethan theatre, and the French stage of the seventeenth century is part of the art of Corneille and Racine. We accept the conventions of our own time without thinking of them, but the influence of these circumstances is just as strong upon Eugene O'Neill as on all his predecessors.

The four great Attic dramatists whose works have come down to us, Aeschylus, Sophocles, Euripides, and Aristophanes, all flourished during the fifth century before Christ. Aeschylus at the age of forty-five fought in the battle of Salamis in 480; Sophocles, as a boy of fifteen, took part in the celebration of the victory; and tradition has it that Euripides was born on the very day of the battle. Aristophanes, the last of the writers of old comedy, was born about the middle of the century, and since the three tragic poets lived to a great old age, all four were practically contemporaries nearly twenty-five hundred years ago. Naturally the conditions under which they wrote at that far time require some explanation today.

We know relatively little about the theatre in the great age of Greek drama—all of the Greek theatres which remain were built long after the dramatists here represented had died. We do know, however, that it was an open-air theatre, its only roof the blue Aegean sky, its only "spot" the clear Aegean sunlight. Perhaps it was for this reason that the scene of all Greek plays was laid out of doors. Directly behind the stage—not a raised platform, probably, but simply levelled ground—stood a temple through which the actors went inside, but all the action which took place in the temple or palace was reported on the stage. Now and then the audience was made directly aware of what was happening within, as when in *Agamemnon* the death-cry of the king is heard from behind closed doors, and a moment later Clytemnestra appears in the doorway, holding the dripping knife. But we are never shown an interior scene. This condition made it necessary for the authors to represent only such scenes as could plausibly take place out of doors. Certainly much more of Athenian life was carried on in the open than we should judge from our own, but even so this condition had a definite effect upon the choosing and handling of the story. Another effect of the outdoor theatre was that the audience was large—perhaps as much as ten or fifteen thousand—and widely diffused; consequently the action presented on the stage had to be simple and impressive, rather than swift and complicated. In the Athenian theatre the finesse of gesture to which we are accustomed would have been obscured by distance, and words spoken in rapid or violent action would never have reached their hearers. So used do we become to our own theatrical conventions that we are likely to overlook the fact that the Athenian stage had no curtain; yet without that simple appliance most of our plays could never be presented. Without curtain or wings or fly, scene shifting was a difficult if not impossible matter, and dramatists, therefore, developed the convention of representing all action as taking place in one spot—what we have come to call the unity of place. When we wish to indicate a lapse of time, we lower the curtain. The Greek dramatist faced the same problem in presenting his action, but he could not use the same solution. Without a curtain, his play had to go on, and he uses the chorus to cover the lapse of time with song and dance. In *Agamemnon,* for instance, between the announcement of the herald and the arrival of the king several days elapse while the chorus is singing its ode.

But this mechanical use of the chorus was only a developed function. Actually the chorus was the heart of the Greek play, and since it is the element strangest to our modern experience, something more must be said about it.

The great Greek religious festivals were those which were solemnized at seed-time and harvest in honor of Demeter and Dionysos, the one the goddess of grain and the other the god of wine. It was a pagan worship which sprang not from a sense of sin, but from a desire to propitiate and thank these two divinities who represented the chief forces of nature. There was about it, therefore, the seriousness which belongs to any honest religion, but there was also a gaiety in its celebration which we do not naturally associate with worship; and from these two spirits, as they were expressed in religious exercises, grew tragedy and comedy. The central element in these festivals was the choral song and dance, which might be either grave and impressive or riotously gay. From the gradual addition of first an interlocutor for the chorus, then a story to furnish the substance of the song, and finally of another actor so that the story might be brought out by dialogue, evolved the dramatic form. At first the play was built about the chorus, as in *The Suppliants* of Aeschylus, where the chorus of the fifty daughters of Danaüs is the protagonist of the drama. Later the chorus was fitted into the story. In *Agamemnon* it is made up of the old men who had been left at home when the Greeks set out for Troy. They have seen the changes wrought by the rule of Clytemnestra, and they feel the imminence of danger to the state, but in the impotence of their age and station they are helpless. The chorus of Oedipus is formed of the plague-stricken citizens of Thebes, whose troubles set Oedipus to inquire into his history, and in whose interest he brings about his own ruin. Gradually the chorus declined in importance until in the last plays of Euripides and Aristophanes it is distinctly secondary, but the real Greek drama could not exist without it. These lyric passages express not only the spirit of the occasion, but the attitude towards life which the chief actors in the story illustrate dramatically.

This rapid summary of the circumstances surrounding the Greek drama of the fifth century B.C. may help to make the form more intelligible, but the strangeness remains. The Greek play was written in poetry, whereas the natural vehicle for ours is prose; its action was simple and impressive, whereas ours tends to be complicated and subtle; it was severely limited as to the number of actors and changes of scene, whereas we are very free in both respects; it was carried on by means of long speeches with little movement, we use shorter, more natural speeches and freer movement; and, finally, the Greek play was built about a chorus for which we have no counterpart whatever. With this knowledge the plays may be more effective as plays, but if the Attic drama could not speak to us without our reconstructing an entirely different civilization, it would be an interesting relic, but in no sense a living voice in modern life.

The permanent appeal of the Attic drama arises from the fact that it presents with the vividness of the greatest art an attitude towards life at once so honest and so intelligent that the minds of men, however far they may be deceived by fancy or philosophy, must always return to it at the end. By virtue of something that looks almost like racial genius the Athenians of the fifth century succeeded in looking upon life with a level gaze. They faced it neither with bravado and bluster, nor with fear and trembling; not

with an ignorant assumption of power over it, nor with an **equally** ignorant and cowardly feeling of inferiority. They found it not always pleasant; in fact more often it was a dark, uncertain battle with the odds against them. "Ah! What is mortal life?" sings the chorus in *Agamemnon,*

> "When prosperous,
> A shadow can o'erturn it, and, when fallen,
> A throw of the wet sponge blurs the picture out."

And again:

> "Who but a god goes woundless all the way?"

But they do not seek to escape the danger, nor complain of the unequal struggle, nor delude themselves with dreams. They accepted life as they found it, not as good or evil, but as a fact and if they questioned, it was How? not Why? They took their plots from old-time legends of the lives of men, and in their dramas they presented life not as it should be, but as it was and is. Their heroes may be good or evil, but the poets are not deluded with a belief in poetic justice. There is no nobler character in literature than Antigone, but her very nobility drives her to destruction. Nor are men made good or evil by force of circumstance. Circumstance may force the tragedy, but the characters are good or evil in their reaction to the circumstances, and the circumstances themselves are not criticized, they are presented. It is a common belief that fate dominates the Greek drama, and that consequently it does not portray men and women as free moral agents. Nothing could be farther from the truth. The Greeks recognized, as we in our moments of wisdom also recognize, that the outcome of man's life is determined by circumstances over which he has no control, but the virtue of his character is a matter quite apart from this and altogether his own affair. The murder of Agamemnon is part of the fulfillment of the curse on the house of Atreus, but Clytemnestra is evil of herself, not made so by fate. The fall of Oedipus is the fulfillment of a prophecy, but Oedipus in his reaction to the circumstances shows himself a good man.

In this courageous acceptance of life as it is, the Greeks succeeded in uniting the passion for truth and the sense of wonder with a completeness to which our only modern parallel is the truly great scientific mind, which will have nothing but truth, and knows that to find truth it must accept, not judge, the facts of nature. The natural result of this honest intellectualism was a serenity of spirit that brings to the end of the most terrible of Greek tragedies, not "consolation," indeed, but "calm of mind all passion spent." Honest intellectualism, and its attendant simplicity and serenity, these are the spiritual content of the four Athenian dramatists; but their manifestation is different with each poet.

. . . .

Aeschylus is the oldest and perhaps the noblest of the dramatists whose word has been preserved. Certainly he is the most severe, and in *Agamemnon* he has presented his story with a dramatic intensity that has never been surpassed in the history of literature. Nowhere, except in the boding beauty of the first scene of *Hamlet,* is there another such opening scene as that which discovers just before the dawn the watchman keeping his year-long vigil upon the Atridae's tower. In a few packed lines he runs the gamut of his emotions during the years of watching, and at the end there flashes on his tired eyes the beacon which tells that Troy is taken at last. He summons the house, but his joy is dimmed by premonitions of disaster, and the chorus of old men, as it recalls the events of the years of waiting, finds it hard to "let the happier note prevail." Clytemnestra enters, queenly and ominous, and the passionate imagery with which she traces the flash of the beacon from headland to headland, even her honeyed words to the herald and the chorus, increases our sense of a tremendous power, not all for good. Even the triumphant Agamemnon scents disaster in the magnificence of his reception, and the wailing figure of the captive Cassandra has scarcely vanished down the crimson carpet when to the trembling chorus comes the death-cry of the king. Here is the climax of the action, but we have yet to see the consummation of evil as Clytemnestra, knife in hand, stands in the doorway, taunting the old men and boasting of her crime. A gorgeous setting, action swift and terrible, and tremendous poetry, all in the shadow of the great Aeschylean idea that:

> "The issue of impious deeds is evil still,
>   With plenteous increase, like to like succeeding."

By the original crime of Atreus in feeding Thyestes a banquet of his own children "the race is wedded to calamity," but the judgment of the chorus is against Clytemnestra:

> "The offence is thine,
>   Whatever spirit of hoarded recompense
>   From elder ages may have wrought with thee."

Evil breeds evil, is the eternal law, but under it the human character is morally responsible. Aeschylus presented men

and women acting under what to him was the funda-
mental law of life; there is criticism of the characters, but
no attempt to explain or justify the law.

In the drama of Sophocles, Aeschylus' younger contemporary, is represented the highest degree of Greek detachment.
He sat, says Tennyson, "like a god, holding no form of
creed, yet contemplating all." He is not primarily concerned with the laws that govern life. With him the first
interest is man—

"Many wonders there be, but naught more wondrous than
    man,"—

and man he represents not in vindication of any moral law,
but as in his strength and weakness he steers his course
through the dark waters of experience. It may or may not
be his fault that he is caught in an eddy and sucked
down—that is of little consequence—what matters is that
he hold his helm steady. The end may be ruinous, but it
is often glorious. Sophocles knew that life is as pitiless to
ignorance as it is to wickedness, and, like a true Greek,
he finds no fault with the fact. He may present man as the
helpless victim of an unjust universe, but his purpose is to
permit us to contemplate the eternal wonder of humanity,
as Pope later described it,

"The glory, jest, and riddle of the world."

Oedipus, as has been said, is a good man: he has shown
himself a wise king, and with the noblest intentions he
pulls down the sky upon his own head. We, who know the
whole story before he does, tremble with expectancy as
step by step he gathers the forces for his own destruction,
and when finally blind and mad, with blood streaming

from his sightless sockets, he rushes from the scene, we sit
transfixt at the malevolent power of circumstance and the
awful capacity of the human soul for suffering. Horror
there is, and pity, but there is also admiration, and most of
all there is wonder, staggering wonder at man and the
ways of man in life. Ibsen in *Rosmersholm* used the same
sort of plot, and there, too, the unravelling of the past
drives the present action to disaster, but with what a difference. Always with Ibsen, society is the villain, there is
something wrong with the universe. Sophocles has no
complaint to make; there is nothing wrong, there is only
what is, and that his play presents.

    With Euripides, the last of the three, there comes another
and greater change. Like Sophocles, he found no law, but
he was worried about it, and his plays are a passionate
vindication of man. Where Aeschylus presented the vindication of the moral law, and Sophocles the wonder and
mystery of man, Euripides plead man's cause against the
forces that destroy him. *Medea* is the story of a woman
wronged. Her story is interesting because she is interesting,
not as it is the story of mankind. It was the nature of
Greek tragedy to present heroic but typical characters in
extraordinary but typical crises. Medea is a strange, exotic
woman in a trying situation, and her solution is entirely
her own. Hers is perhaps the most terrible display of passion in literature, but it lacks the universality characteristic
of Greek drama. The old Greek tragedy was clearly
changing in the hands of Euripides, and that, no doubt,
accounts for his contemporary failure—he won only five
first prizes in a long life, notwithstanding that he was
ranked as the first poet in Greece. His reward has been to
become the most popular Greek dramatist to modern
readers.

With Aristophanes we have another end, but for us he is also a beginning. He was the last of the writers of the old comedy, and he is the only one whose work has been preserved. The old comedy of Athens is tragedy with a grinning face; not that it is burlesque of the great themes, or even structurally resembles tragedy, but Greek comedy is simply that same honest intellectualism used in the interests of laughter.

Comedy, by its very nature, is intellectual. The comic muse had reason for her handmaid, as the tragic muse has passion. One can feel without thinking—in fact one usually does—but one cannot recognize an incongruity even of the most obvious sort without the exercise of reason. It is only natural, that when the comic spirit took hold of a people as intellectual as the Athenians of the fifth century it raised peals of laughter such as have rarely been heard since. It was another aspect of their passion for truth that the comic spirit should be free. Nothing and no one was safe from it; war and philosophy, poets, statesmen, tradesmen, slaves, and women of every variety were victims of the jibes of Aristophanes. He did not hesitate to smother with ridicule the greatest man in Athens or the last solemn undertaking of the state. He is the spirit of Dionysos, wine and spring and the riotous joy of the free creative impulse, and his only serious purpose is to raise a laugh. His comedy is intellectual, but it makes no snobbish pretense. He knew that slapstick is funny and that there can be a hearty laugh without viciousness in a lewd situation, and he used both with a verve and audacity that sweeps away all moral objections. With all his coarseness there is not a speck of moral pollution in Aristophanes. He is the great mind at play, turning the world upside down for the fun of it as Rabelais did, but all with a polished art to which Rabelais was a stranger. We cannot produce in English the lyric beauty of his verse, but he is the supreme example of the master poet turned clown. "Monkeys and nightingales in the tree-tops," has been given as the symbol of his spirit; for us the antics of the monkeys remain, but only the faintest echo of the song of the bird.

.   .   .   .

This is the message of the Attic drama—this honest intellectualism, this passion for truth, this serene and level gaze on life—and this has always been the modern spirit. For seven hundred years, ever since the first glimmer of the Renaissance, great spirits here and there have been struggling to make it prevail. It is the struggle to free the intellect, to tear from it the veils of hope and fear, so that it may look clearly and unafraid upon the face of life and know it as it is, terrible and pitiful and glorious and utterly nonsensical. Once for a short time in Athens twenty-five hundred years ago this vision was achieved, and from that brilliant age rise the tragic figures of kings and queens to show what men saw in it: the stifled cry of Agamemnon from behind the palace doors; Cassandra praying for the fate of the ever-mournful nightingale; blind Oedipus, once more a king at heart, walking out alone from Colonus to vanish from the world; and lest the spirit of man grow too proud with the dignity of sorrow, from the reeds along the river Styx comes the mocking chorus of the Frogs.

PAUL LANDIS

URBANA, ILLINOIS,
January, 1929.

AGAMEMNON

BY

AESCHYLUS

PERSONS OF THE DRAMA

A Watchman.
Chorus *of the Argive Elders.*
Clytemnestra.
Herald.
Agamemnon.
Cassandra.
Aegisthus.

Scene—Argos, before the palace of the Atridae.

Time—After the fall of Troy.

ARGUMENT

ARGOS is still the metropolis of Hellas, and the palace is occupied by the two sons of Atreus, Agamemnon and Menelaus, as joint kings. They have married sisters, Clytemnestra and Helenè, daughters of Tyndareus. But Helen has been carried off by Paris, and the two brothers are described as having together departed on the Trojan expedition. But the fleet was delayed at Aulis, and Agamemnon was induced to sacrifice his daughter Iphigenia, or Iphianassa. This act has awakened an inextinguishable hatred in the breast of her mother Clytemnestra, who remains in sole possession of the vast palace of the Pelopidae—that home which has already witnessed the banquet of Thyestes and other nameless iniquities. She sends away her son Orestes, and, amongst the horror-breathing silences, remains alone, possessed with the one thought, the one constant resolve, to take condign vengeance for her child.

But while alone in the palace, she is not alone in her desire of revenge. Aegisthus, the son of Thyestes, is bound in honour to be avenged for his brothers, whom Atreus massacred. He has returned to Argolis, but is still an outcast from the palace of the Pelopidae.

During the absence of Agamemnon and Menelaus these two hatreds have coalesced in one,—Clytemnestra, reckless of all but vengeance, Aegisthus, likewise loving revenge but not insensible to the charms of the kingdom and the Queen.

Their plot is favoured by the circumstance that, when Agamemnon returns, his brother Menelaus is still absent, having been intercepted by a violent storm. Although suspicion is rife, there has been no overt act either of adultery

3

or usurpation. But after one of his secret visits, **Aegisthus** has left with Clytemnestra his sword. (Choeph. 1008.)

After entangling her husband in the rich hangings, **or** carpetings, over which she has persuaded him to walk **in** entering the palace, the Queen dispatches him with the sword of Aegisthus.

The King had brought home with him Cassandra, the daughter of Priam. This insult serves to whet the Queen's revenge. And the character of the prophetic maiden, her destined victim, stands in pathetic contrast to that of the royal murderess.

The King's death-shriek is, of course, the crisis of the play, and more than justifies the gloomy presentiments which damp all attempts at cheerfulness on the part of the Watchman, the Chorus, and the Herald. For this culminating horror the mind of the spectator has been further prepared, first by certain lurid flashes of Clytemnestra's demoniac joy, and then by a scene in which the growing apprehension of the event is mingled with the most poignant tenderness of pity, as Cassandra, the captive princess, whom Apollo has inspired and forsaken, prophetically describes both the past abominations of the house of Atreus, and the cruel **doom** that is immediately impending over Agamemnon and herself.

AGAMEMNON

WATCHMAN

I ASK the gods deliverance from the toil
Of these long watchings. Through twelve weary moons
Couched on the Atridae's house-top, like a dog,
With head on hand, and ever-wakeful eye,
I have conned the nightly concourse of the stars
That shine majestical in yon clear heaven,
And by their risings and their settings bring
Summer and winter to the world. To-night
I watch for the flame-signal that shall tell
To us in Argos tidings borne from Troy,
Voicing her capture. Such the strong command
Of an expectant, passionate, man-souled woman.
This bed of mine beneath the dews of night
Conduces not to rest. Dreams come not near it.
Else they are warned off by the sentinel Fear,
That will not let my lids securely close.
Then if I whistle, or soothe a tune, providing
Such antidote 'gainst slumber, my sad heart
Checks me with groans for the calamities
That haunt this house,—not guided for the best
As once it was.—Well! may the nightly flame
Soon, with glad news, release me from my toil.

[*The beacon is seen.*

All hail! thou light in darkness, harbinger
Of day indeed, author of many a song

5

And dance in Argos, born of this event!
Solá, solá!
I cry aloud to Agamemnon's queen
That from her couch she spring with speed, and raise
Clamour of joy to hail this beacon-light,
For Troy is taken; so the fires declare.
Nay, I'll begin, and dance by way of prelude.
Marking my master's game, I'll cry 'Huzzá!
Good luck! Three sixes, thrown by Bonfire-blaze!'-
Good luck, do I say? 'Twill be some joy to hold
The kind hand of this kingdom's lord in mine.
Beyond that, I am silent. A strange weight
Oppresses heart and tongue. Could the house speak,
It might have much to tell. My lips will open,
With my good will, only to those that know.

CHORUS (*entering*)

Nine years are gone, and the tenth is here,
Since he whom Priam had cause to fear,
Menelaus, wreaking a mighty wrong,
And Agamemnon, in glory strong,
With twofold sceptre and throne secure
Gifted by Him whose gifts are sure—
Two sons of Atreus leagued in power,
Of Argive youth led forth the flower,
Well armed for aid, the Aegean o'er,
In a thousand ships from yonder shore.

Shouting they went, with hearts aflame
For the furious War-god's eager game.
Like eagles, that over their eyrie wheel,
Driven wide by the sudden pang they feel
For their eaglets torn from the long-watched nest,

Oaring their path in wild unrest
With pens for oar-blades,—till one on high,
Pan or Apollo, hearing the cry
Of the birds who tenant his realm of air,
Is moved by the sound of their shrill despair,
And sends on the sinner, albeit too late,
To redress that wrong, an avenging fate.

So mightier Zeus, who guards the home
From outrage of guests that idly roam,
'Gainst Paris both the Atridae brought,
For a woman, whose marriage vows were naught,
Broaching a flood of toils, to flow
For Greek and Trojan with equal woe,—
When the knee outwearied should press the dust,
And the spear be snapped in the virgin thrust.—
Each hour hath proof of the daily state,
But the end shall be as 'tis ruled by Fate.
No late libation, or incense-fume,
Avails to save from a ruthless doom
The man who has angered, through mad desire,
The Powers that burn, but need no fire.
Now we, discarded through Time's decay,
Dropt from the roll that mustering day,
Remain, supporting, as weakness craves,
Our child-like gait upon walking-staves.
For the sap that sprang in our breasts of yore
Knows of his youthful might no more,
And the warlike spirit hath left his seat.
What task for withering Eld is meet?
Doting, he wanders his three-foot way,
Proving such valour as children may,
Of no more strength than a dream in the day.

But thou, Clytemnestra, royal dame,
What cause hath kindled thine altar-flame?
What new hath fallen? What tidings heard
With sudden motion thy heart have stirred,
To raise by thy missives ranging wide
Frankincense fuming on every side?
Of all the gods that in Argos dwell,
Gods of Olympus, and gods of Hell,
Gods of the palace, gods of the street,
Gods who preside where the people meet,
Where'er is harboured a power divine,
Thy gifts are blazing at every shrine.
Here, there, and yonder, on high doth spire
With holy meaning the fragrant fire,
Fed with rich oils, that mildly soothe
Our doubtful hearts with warrant of truth:
Since the royal perfume with potent spell
From the palace whispers that all is well.—
Whate'er thou mayest, to our minds reveal,
O queen, of thy bounty, and timely heal
Our heart's foreboding, that riseth still
One while with thoughts of impending ill,
Till Hope, appearing with kindly light
From the altar, greets our reviving sight,
And strives to banish the carking care
That fiercely feeds on the soul's despair.

Full power is mine to sing what heartening sign
    Ushered the flower of warriors on their way:—
Yet soars my spirit; yet, from springs divine,
    Life yields me valour to uplift the lay,
        Telling how, on a day,
The king of birds marshalled two kings of men,—

Joint leaders of the youth of Hellas, then
On ship-board led against the Teucrian land
With store of vengeance in each spear-armed hand:—
A warlike sign! Two eagles on the right:
        Full in the army's sight,
Hard by yon royal roof they took their place
    (One black in all his plumes, one flecked with white),
Gorging together on a brooding hare,
    O'ertaken in her latest chase,
        A creature of despair!
Then be your burden sad with sounds of wail,
    But let the happier note prevail.

The careful prophet saw the Atridae twain,
    And straightway in the hare-devourers scanned
Those warlike leaders with their differing strain;
    Then thus he spake prophetic: 'Yonder band
        In time shall take the land
Of royal Priam: and the public store
Wherewith the towers of Troy were filled before,
Stern fate through violent shocks of armèd power
Shall pitilessly ransack and devour.
Only, may no offence from Heaven distain
        The bridle of Ilion's plain,
That brilliant army, crossed by heavenly ire!
Since holiest Artemis, with wrath o'erta'en,
Frowns as they feast on yon poor trembler's brood,
    Those wingèd minions of her Sire.
        She abhors the eagles' food.'
Then be your burden sad with sounds of wail,
    But let the happier note prevail.

'The beauteous goddess, though so kind
    To eanlings of the ravening lion-race,

And tender sucklings of all beasts of chase,
    Doth yet accord her mind
To fair fulfilment of the favouring sign.
Ah! but on Phoebus yet I call,
    Healer in dangers all,
Lest for the Argives, with intent malign,
She raise contrarious winds of dire delay,
    Minded another victim to exchange
    In sacrifice unauthorized and strange,
    Attended with no festival,
    Breeding dark strife within the hall,
Hardening the wife against the husband's sway.
A mindful keeper of the house shall burn
To avenge her offspring at her lord's return.'
Such words of doom, mingled with fortunate things,
Calchas outspake, touching our race of kings.
Then be your burden sad with sounds of wail
    But let the happier note prevail.

    Zeus—by what name soe'er
        He glories being addressed,
    Even by that holiest name
        I name the Highest and Best.
    On Him I cast my troublous care,
    My only refuge from despair:
Weighing all else, in Him alone I find
Relief from this vain burden of the mind.

    One erst appeared supreme,
        Bold with abounding might,
    But like a darkling dream
        Vanished in long past night,
    Powerless to save; and he is gone
    Who flourished since, in turn to own

His conqueror, to whom with soul on fire
Man crying aloud shall gain his heart's desire,—

> Zeus, who prepared for men
>   The path of wisdom, binding fast
> Learning to suffering. In their sleep
>   The mind is visited again
> With memory of affliction past.
>   Without the will, reflection deep
> Reads lessons that perforce shall last,
Thanks to the power that wields the sovran oar,
Resistless, toward the eternal shore.

> And the elder leader then
>   Of all the Achaeans, blaming not
> The prophet, but with quivering lips
>   Bending his spirit to the strain
> Of that unlooked-for, adverse lot,—
>   What time the Achaeans by their ships
> Were sore distressed with anxious thought,
By baffling winds, that drained that opulent host,
Storm-stayed on Aulis' weary coast.

For fronting Chalkis' bay,
Helpless as logs the Achaean galleys lay;
While blasts of dire delay from Strymon's mouth,
Authors of hunger, weariness and drouth,
Driving poor wights from hospitable shores,
Doubling the loss of time through waste of stores,
Sparing nor ships nor cordage, wore away
The flower of Argive youth.—
And when the prophet cried,
Voicing a plan to cure the army's pain,

Even than that cruel wind
More cruel to the chieftains in their pride,
Recalling Artemis to mind,
Whereat the Atridae with their sceptres twain
Striking the ground, from tears could not refrain;

' 'Twere hard to disobey,'
These words the elder chieftain spake that day,
'But were 't not hard on the altar-step to stand
And stain with virgin streams a father's hand?
O heavy doom! if I my child must slay,
Who sheds upon my home its brightest ray!
Which way I turn is fraught with evil still,
No course exempt from ill.
How should I fail the fleet?
How sin against the bond myself impressed?
This blood will stay the storm:
Then for the blood of maiden pure and sweet,
The ruin of a faultless form,
Sorrow must yield to passionate unrest
Of strong desire. May all be for the best!'

So when his neck received the fatal yoke,
Within his breast arose the counter-gale,
And impious thoughts from lurking depths upbroke,
        Unholy and fraught with bale.
An altered man, he recked no more of crime.
For the first shock of grief bore unfelt
Hardens the spirit, that erewhile could melt,
With maddening counsel. He, that dreadful time,
Endured to slay his daughter, so to aid
The warfare in a woman's cause arrayed,—
        So to advance the fleet
        With favouring auspice meet!

What cared that council, eager for the strife,
That on her lip the name of father hung,
That unpolluted was her virgin life,
   So pure, so bright, so young!
The father bade those priests, after the prayer,
Above the altar, face to earth, on high,
Like kindling there to lift her ruthlessly,
With garments drooping round her, and the fair
Sweet mouth to bridle with speech-stifling force.
Lest some faint cry, heard in that ritual's course,
      Might bring disastrous doom
      Upon her father's home.

She shed to earth her veil of saffron dye,
And smote her sacrificers one by one
With pity-kindling arrows from her eye,
Willing to speak, as if some artist hand
That dumb fair piece had done.
How often in her own dear land
She charmed the feasters in her father's hall,
With fresh young voice honouring his festival,
And with her loving presence graced the store
Of scathless plenty on that palace-floor!

What followed then I saw not, nor will tell;
The mystic arts of Calchas won their way.
Nor on things future boots it now to dwell;
Farewell to that!   Clear, in the history's close,
'Twill dawn with the new day.
Knowledge belongs of right to those
Who read the lesson of the fact they feel.
Fore-thinking were fore-sorrowing. May the wheel
Bring round good fortune! such the wishful mind
Of us, last guards of Argos left behind.

Enter CLYTEMNESTRA

LEADER OF CHO. Queen Clytemnestra, we are come to render
Our duties to thy royalty. For when
The kingly throne is vacant, it is meet
The consort of the prince should have all homage.
We are here with loyal hearts intent to learn
If some good tidings coming to thine ear
Have prompted thine auspicious sacrifice.
Speak, if thou wilt. If not, we rest content.

CLY. 'With glad intelligence,' the proverb saith,
'Let Morning issue from the womb of Night.'
A joy beyond your hope 'tis yours to hear.
Our Argive host hath taken Priam's town.

CHO. How? 'Tis incredible. Speak yet again.

CLY. Troy is in Grecian hands. Are those words plain?

CHO. Unlooked for joy brings tears into mine eye.

CLY. Those tears attest your loyalty of heart.

CHO. But hast thou proof that may be trusted, lady?

CLY. Unless some god have been deceiving me.

CHO. Hast thou then hearkened to some flattering dream?

CLY. No slumbrous fancies work on my belief.

CHO. But some speech-omen, lighting on thy soul—

CLY. Should that elate me like a girl? Ye mock me!

CHO. Say, then, how long ago the city fell.

CLY. In the same night that now brings forth the day.

CHO. What messenger could bear the news so swiftly?

CLY. The Fire-god flashed it hither from Mount Ida.
Fire was the post, and beacons were the stages.
First Ida sent him to the Hermaean bluff
Of Lemnos, whence the flaming torch that rose

Was caught by Athos, Zeus's promontory;
Thence high aloft, far-glancing o'er the sea,
The blazing pine sped on the traveller-flame,
Making strange sunrise on Makistus' height,
Who, ready for that dawn, neglected not
A courier's office, but gave signal far
Across Euripus to the watchmen set
On wild Messapius. They replied and sent
The glad news onward, kindling a dry heap
Of agèd heather. And the mighty flame,
Nought bating of his radiant power, o'erleapt
Asopus' flats, and, like a brilliant moon
Silvering the forehead of Cithaeron, waked
A fresh relay of courier torches there:
Nor was the far-sped beacon-flame denied;
But re-inforcing it beyond command,
That mountain guard upreared a royal blaze,
To shoot beyond Gorgopis' bay and strike
The mount of Aegiplanctus, where it roused
Loyal renewal of the appointed fire.
Heaping on fuel with unsparing hand,
They raised a beard-like pyramid of flame,
Whose light rushed past the foreland that looks forth
Towards Aegina, till it reached the height
That crowns our city, this Arachnian hill:—
Whence, lastly, on the Atridae's roof lights down
That lineal offspring of the Idaean flame.
Such torch-race had we ordered and prepared,
In bright successive courses ministered.
But here one runner, first and last i' the race,
Hath touched the goal and shouted 'Victory!'
This is the proof and token I proclaim,
Sent by my husband from the heart of Troy.

Сно.   O lady, our thanksgivings shall be paid
To Heaven, hereafter. We would hear thee still,
Listening and wondering,—so thou wouldst speak anew.
    Cly.   To-day the Achaeans are possessed of Troy.
A jarring din, methinks, is rising there!
Into one vessel pouring oil and vinegar
You will not see them lovingly combine.
Even so the captives' and the captors' cries
Tell diverse tales of Fortune's twofold power.
Those now are fallen about the prostrate forms
Of husbands, brothers, friends,—young children, too,
Clinging to grey-haired fathers,—and from throats
No longer free, lament their dearest slain.
But these, being wearied with the night's exploit,
O'er-watched and hungry, break their fast i' the town
On what is yet to be found there,—not by rule—
No order, no precedence, no degree,—
But even as each hath plucked the lot of chance.
So now inhabiting the ransacked homes
Of captive Trojans, sheltered from the dews
And frosts of the open field, as men released
From toil, they will sleep all night, nor dream of danger
And if they reverence well the gods that hold
The captured city, and the temples there,
The spoiler may escape being spoiled. But let
No lust seduce that host to plunder things
Inviolable, as overcome by greed.
The race is not yet over. Still remains
The home-return, to round their emulous course.
Yea, even without offended Deity.
Or tricks of chance, the spirits of the slain
May awake in wrath and bar the homeward way.
Thus,—if ye list to hear a woman's word,—

Would run my counsel. But may good prevail
Without a flaw! The blessings of my home
Are manifold, and I would keep them still.

[*Exit* CLYTEMNESTRA

LEADER OF CHO. All praise to thee, Zeus, king supreme!
and, O night, kind protectress, to thee!
How rich were thy splendours, when over the bulwarks
of Troy
Thou didst drop the wide net of destruction, that none,
great or small, man or boy,
Fled beyond, but was taken or perished, none crept through
the meshes of doom.
All praise to the power everlasting that punishes perfidy
home!
Long since on the string was the arrow, that neither too
fleebly should fly,
Nor idly o'er head of the sinner should mount, as if aimed
at the sky,
But should pierce through the bosom of Paris.—The hour
and the death-stroke are come!

CHORUS

From Zeus came down the stroke that lowered their pride.
So much may be discerned beyond dispute.
They fared as he determined. One denied
Gods could be thought to care, when man or brute
Had trampled o'er the grace of holiest things.
He knew not reverence. But the truth is shown
In judgement falling on proud warrior-kings
Who, when their halls were bursting with excess
Beyond the limit of true happiness,
Defied all laws to gods or mortals known.

Zeus punishes mortal impiety and pride.

Where is the limit?   Let but sorrow cease
And all within be peace,
The wise in heart shall be well satisfied.
For wealth ne'er proved a fortress for the man
Who, mad with having, insolently ran
At Right's high altar, in his impious thought
Minded to hurl it into nought.

But strong Delusion, Sin's disastrous child,
Brooding o'er future trespass, works her will
Remediless.   Not to be reconciled
Nor yet concealed, the bane is shining still,
As in the assaying peers the base alloy,
With lurid brilliance ruinously clear.
Even so he fares, who, like a wanton boy,
Chases the bird that mocks his eager hand,
And on his people brings a cureless brand.
Loudly he prays, but none in Heaven will hear.
God strikes to earth the man of unjust ways,
Outcast from hope of praise.
So Paris, harboured in these halls, defiled
With base ingratitude the Atridae's home.
He wronged the chieftain of yon stately dome,
Stealing with robber guile the beauteous wife,
Unfaithful cause of future strife.

She left unto her friends in Argos here
Clashing of shields, arming of ships and men,
And, taking to the city of her new lord
Destruction for a dowry, lightly then
She passed the portal, sinning without fear,
Whilst ominous voices there that flight deplored:
'Woe for the palace home!   Woe for her spouse!
Woe for her wifely ways within the house!

He stands dishonoured, silent, murmuring not,
Soul-stricken before that unremovèd blot,
While longing for the lost one over seas
Shall banish all heart's-ease,
That some unbodied ghost shall seem
To rule the house, as in a dream.
The loveliest forms of stone
To that deserted one
Are hateful. In the spirit's listless void
All sense of beauty sinks destroyed.

'Yet visions of the night, born of regret,
Bring to his saddened soul a vain delight.
Is it not vain if, when one thinks to reap
Strange joy, the cherished object fleets from sight
(Even while with gladdening tears the eyes are wet)
On wings that follow with the steps of sleep?'
Such homefelt wounds within the palace wall
Are bleeding. Ay, and would that these were all!—
Nay, everywhere through Grecian lands is seen,
In each man's home, much heart-corroding teen.
From Grecian lands together forth they went,
Each by their loved ones sent,
And now the soul of friends is sore
To think whom they shall see no more.
Whom they sent forth they know,
But to their bitter woe,
No well-loved form, but urns of crumbling earth
Return to each man's natal hearth.

Ares, grim usurer of blood and breath,
That swings his balance o'er the fields of death,
Sends back from Ilium to their friends
(For warriors' loss no just amends)

Their ashes blackened by the funeral fire,—
Poor dust! so heavy not with gold but grief,
Affording to the dumb desire
Of tears but scant relief.
Then as with tender heed they store away
Each precious burden in its vase of clay,
They groan, while praising one for skill in fight
And one for his brave conduct in the strife,
'Fallen to avenge another warrior's wife.'
This last is murmured low,
While silent wrath doth grow
'Gainst Atreus' sons, great champions of their right.
Others, with limbs unravaged, in the shade
By Ilion's bulwarks made,
Rest undisturbed;—the hostile land they hold
Hides them beneath her kindly mould.
Ah! dangerous are the murmurs of the town!
A nation's curse lives in the people's frown.
One thought of mine night yet doth shroud:
It would be spoken, but not loud:
Great bloodshed draws the gaze of Deity.
The dark Erinys in long lapse of time
Grinds down to helpless poverty
Him who in ways of crime
Hath flourished, but in dim reverse of doom
Shall stain the lustre of that odious bloom;
And, once among the lost, he hath no more force.
Danger is theirs, too, that are praised by all:
From jealous eyes the fire of Heaven doth fall.
Mine be the moderate lot
That envy blasteth not!
I would not run the royal conqueror's course,

Nor yet would I be conquered, and behold
The life I shared of old
Subdued to strangers, and my country's folk
Writhing beneath an alien yoke.

Good news delivered by the beacon flash
Shot through the city a rumour swift and rash,
Yet who can tell if things be as they seem,
Or God have sent us a deceitful gleam?
'Twere childish or insensate to allow
One's heart to kindle at that cheering glow,
      And quench it when a word
      Of differing note is heard.

None but a woman, framed of hopes and fears,
Should yield assent before the fact appears.
Persuasion soon invades the female's realm:
Her judgment's pale is quickly overthrown;
Feebly she holds an unresisting helm:
But fading soon to nothing the renown
      Told by a woman's tongue
      Will not endure for long.

Enter the HERALD

LEADER OF CHO. Ha!
Now we shall know for certain how to deem
Of those bright signals of transmitted fire,
Whether truth is in them, or this light of joy,
Dreamlike, cajoled our minds with empty hope.
I see a herald coming from the shore
With olive-boughs o'ershadowed, and the dust
(Clay's thirsty neighbouring sister) tells me plain
This is no voiceless phantom-messenger

Of smoke and blaze from mountain bonfire sprung,
But will speak audibly,—whether of joy,
Or—but I waive the less auspicious word.
May that fair token now be crowned with good!—
Whoso prays otherwise for this our state,
Heaven visits his soul's trespass on himself.

HER. O Fatherland of Argos, dearly loved,
In this tenth year I tread thy hallowed ground:
Though many a hope hath snapped, this anchor holds
Beyond expectance. I had long despaired
E'en of kind burial in my native earth.
Hail, Argive country, Argive light, and thou,
Zeus over all!—thou too, great Pythian king,
Let thy keen darts no longer fly our way.
Enough they vexed us before Troy. But now,
Apollo, heal and save us! Yea, all ye
Gods of our thoroughfares,—thou above all,
Hermes, dear herald, whom we heralds worship,—
And ye, great warriors of old time, whose spirits
Followed us forth,—receive again from war
With kindly thoughts this remnant of the host.
O well-loved palace of our kings, and ye,
Dread thrones of judgement, and great Powers that face
The morning, with your brightest glances greet
Our Sovereign in his triumph of to-day.
He comes, long waited for, bringing to you
And all this people glory out of gloom,
Light for long darkness. Then salute him well
Who well deserves it, having ransacked Troy,
And dug the ground there with the spade of Doom,
That, by the righteous will of Zeus most high,
Temples and altars are no more, no more
A germ of life in all the desolate land.

Such yoke is cast upon proud Ilion's neck
By the elder son of Atreus, who this day
Returns, a happy warrior, of all men
Most to be honoured, having wreaked in full
The rape of Helen on all the Trojan name.
Not Paris, or all his people leagued in one,
May boast their suffering lighter than their deed.
Proclaimed a thief and robber, he hath lost
More than his booty, having razed to the earth
His father's house and ravaged his own land.
Priam's sons have paid the penalty twice o'er.

CHO. Hail! herald of the host; I bid thee joy.
HER. Yea; from this moment I could welcome death.
CHO. Didst thou so yearn for this thy fatherland?
HER. So that warm tears stand in mine eyes for glad-
    ness.
CHO. Then in that trouble ye were not unblest.
HER. Let me be master of that speech. Explain.
CHO. Being touched with love of those who longed for
    you.
HER. Mean you the land yearned likewise for her sons?
CHO. Ay! these dim souls have often sighed for you.
HER. Whence came this cloud upon your spirits? Tell!
CHO. Silence hath long been our best remedy.
HER. How? Feared ye any man, your lord away?
CHO. In thine own words—we could have welcomed
    death.
HER. I spake that in my joy. Yet looking backward,
Doubtless, our hap was chequered with some woe.
Who, save the gods, eternally command
Pleasure unmingled? Were I now to tell
Our toils and hardships 'neath the open sky,
Lying on narrow bunks, ill-lined and bare,

Lamenting each day's lack of every store;
Then on firm land, still worse, to lodge i' the field,
Close under the enemy's wall, with rain from heaven
Or dews from the damp meadow, drizzling over
Our clothes, our bodies, and our clotted hair:—
Or should one tell o' the storm-wind, striking down
The falcon from her pride, with icy power
Swooping from Ida's snows; or of the heat,
When idle Ocean in his bed at noon
Lay motionless, and not an air might breathe—
But no! Why grieve o'er troubles that are past?—
So past for some, as never any more
They will care to rise from where they lie. But we,
The living, why should we to-day count over
The lost, or mourn malignant Fortune's power?
Farewell, say I, to sorrow! We survive;
Our gain o'erweighs past trouble, and to-day
On land, or coursing over seas, we call
This morning's sun to look upon the host
Returning with triumphant spoils from Troy,
By us at length subdued,—to hang them up
In all the temples of Hellenic gods
A bright and everlasting monument.
Hear this, ye people, and extol your State
And our great leaders, duly rendering praise
To Zeus, first author of these gifts. I have said.

Enter CLYTEMNESTRA

CHO. Your happy tidings have prevailed to cheer me.
The old are ever young enough to learn
When good approaches. And thy words bring good,
To our queen and palace first, and then to me.
    CLY. Long since I raised the shout of joy, when came

The first night-messenger of fire to tell
That Troy was taken, Ilion overthrown.
Men chid me, saying, 'Dost thou now believe,
Persuaded by a bonfire, Troy is fallen?
How like a woman to be thus elate!'
Yet brought I mine oblation, and glad cries
In female notes were sounded here and there
About the city,—as with incense poured
They soothed, at every shrine, the odorous flame.
Now, why ask more of thee? I shall hear all
From mine own husband when he comes. I will haste
Nobly to meet my lord's return. What light
Is sweeter to a woman's eyes than that
Which floods the opening gate when Heaven brings home
Her husband from the war? Bear back this word.
Let him come quickly, loved of all the land.
And may he find the wife he left behind
Unchanged, still faithful; watching o'er his home,
Like a good house-dog, fierce to his enemies,
But kind to him; and holding unprofaned
So long, the pressure of his last embrace.
Of joys with other men, or guilty word,
I know no more than of the blacksmith's art.
Such boast, instinct with honest truthfulness,
A noble wife may utter without blame.

[*Exit*

Cho. Herald, thine ear, a sound interpreter,
Hath taught thee the fair meanings of the queen.
But tell us now, we pray thee, of the prince
This land delights to honour, Menelaus,—
Comes he with you in safety to his home?
Her. Were I to utter false glad tidings here,

Short-lived were that delight for those I love.

CHO. Ah then! let what is good be likewise true!
Goodness and truth dissevered are soon known.

HER. I tell the simple truth. The man is lost,
Gone from the fleet. His ship is no more seen.

CHO. Say, launched he forth from Troy in sight of men,
Or did a storm, that troubled all your host,
Snatch him away?

HER.   You hit the centre there,
Condensing in brief words a world of woe.

CHO. How? What report from other mariners
Was noised about him as alive or dead?

HER. One only can with surety answer you,
The Sun, who nourishes Earth's various brood.

CHO. How mean you that the storm assailed the fleet
And proved the exécutor of wrath from Heaven?

HER. A day of blessing ought not to be stained
With news of bale. Heaven's honour should be clear.
An evil messenger with darkened brow
That brought you tidings of an army's fall,
A twofold horror, doubly charged with woe,
First for the country's wound, then for the homes
Whose men had been devoted to the scourge
Loved of the War-god, armed with death and dole—
The tongue so laden with calamities
Might chant this hymn of heavenly wrath.

                                              But I,
Who come with news of peace and bright success
To a city smiling with prosperity,
Why must I dash my good with ill, by telling
Of the dire storm Heaven sent to plague our fleet?
Fire and the sea, those ancient foes, were leagued
In firm alliance visibly fulfilled

To wreck our ill-starred navy. 'Twas i' the night
Came the onset of the billowy adversary,
Big with disaster, for the Thracian blast
Smote ship 'gainst ship, that gored and butted each
Her neighbour, buffeted with swilling brine
And raging tempest, till they passed from sight
Like kine a madman drives. On that wild scene
The sun arising cloudless, showed us all
The Aegean strewn with wreaths of floating wreck,
And bodies of Achaean men. Our vessel,
Some power divine, or pleading with the storm
Or thwarting him, made scathless. 'Twas no mariner,
But saving Providence, stood by our helm,
And steered us, neither to a boisterous road-stead,
Nor on the breakers of a rock-lanced shore.
Then, rescued from that watery death, amidst
Fair daylight, not believing our escape,
Our thoughts were mindful of a new distress,
Mourning the wreck and havoc of our fleet.
May Heaven still work us good! So much is clear.
If any of those we parted from still breathe,
They reason of our death as we of theirs.
And as for Menelaus, let us hope
He above all may be preserved, and come
Back to his home. Zeus wills not yet, we trust,
His race should perish,—and will find some means
To keep him still in life. Somewhere the sun
Beholds him, and his eyes enjoy the day.
Now, Argives, I have told you all the truth.

CHORUS

Who gave the ill-omened name,
So fraught with terror for the time to be,

So true to her career of blame?
War-won, war-wed, war-wakening Helenè?
Was he some prophet-spirit unknown to fame,
    With sure presentiment
    Fore-speaking Time's event?
The name of Helen tells of ships aflame,
    Of souls to Hades sent,
Of countries ravaged, cities overthrown.
        From out the delicately curtained bower,
        Borne by the West-wind's earthborn power,
In Paris' nimble galley forth she went,
        And when they touched on Simois' shore,
With cytisus and myrtle overgrown,
    A many-shielded pack
    Following the viewless track
    Of their swift oar,
Came bent on slaughterous feud and fierce arbitrament.

        That *bond,* so rightly styled,
Bound Ilium with a chain of endless care,
        Sent by some spirit of anger wild
Resolved on ruin, minded to prepare
Revenge for hospitality defiled
        On those who sang that day
        The lawless marriage-lay,
Provoking wrath hard to be reconciled.
        Her new-found brethren gay
Thought not if Zeus approved the enforcèd song.
        Now they and theirs have learned a different strain,
        And Priam's ancient town with pain
Groans heavily from forth her ashes grey,
        Calling on Paris the accurst,
The guilty cause of unforgiven wrong;—

She that in wild despair
For generations fair
Herself had nursed,
Had spent long years of wailing 'midst the fray.

What image fits Troy's fall?
A man, I will say,
Cherished within his hall
A cub, for play,
Just weaned, but hardly, from the lioness.
The prelude of his life
Was far from cruel strife;
The darling of young boys, a thing of sportiveness!
Even old men felt the charm;
Oft in the nestling arm
'Twas dandled, like to human babyhood;
When stroked, he made reply
With fondly brightening eye;
When hunger pressed, he crouched and fawned for food.

But as with time he grew
He showed his stock,
And with dire outrage slew
The home-bred flock,
So making ill return for all that care;
Till all the peaceful floor
With blood was dabbled o'er:
The household slaves beheld in mute despair.
The self-provided feast
Of that unbidden guest
Spread havoc round him wheresoe'er he moved.
Sent by some god to earth
To plague a sinful hearth,
A priest of Atè's self that nursling proved.

Even so methinks there came to Troia's town,
  One tempered like the calm on windless seas,
A face to smite the soul but ne'er to frown,
  A joy luxurious, crowning wealth with ease.
Love there in bloom entranced the passionate mind.
  But soon she turned and made a bitter end
Of nuptial, in old Ilion's hour of need;
  By Zeus who punisheth where guests offend
Brought thither as a bane to Priam's seed:
Kinship unblest! Companionship unkind,
Sad bride of tears, fell fury unconfined!

Wise lips declared, and 'tis an agèd saw,
  That man's prosperity, maturely grown,
Hath offspring that succeeds by Heaven's high law,—
  From happy fortune misery full-blown:
A different thought by me shall be confessed;
  The issue of impious deeds is evil still,
With plenteous increase, like to like succeeding;
  Not so begets its race the righteous will,
But the fair life fair fortune aye is breeding.
No evil brood disturbs that peaceful nest.
The house of the upright evermore is blest.

The pride of former years engendereth pride
  Youngly insulting o'er calamity;
Or soon or late, what matters? When the tide
  Of time brings on the day of destiny
For that fell birth, even then is born the Power,
Unblest, resistless, making warriors cower,
Infatuate Boldness, whose o'ershadowing gloom
Veils all the house with darkness of the tomb;
Such parentage hath bloomed in such fell flower.

The light of Righteousness in smoky homes
  Shines unimpaired, honouring the humble lot;
From gilded halls impure, as Earth she roams,
  She turns her gaze to bless the pious cot;
The power of riches falsely stampt with praise
Wins not her worship by its spurious blaze;
Her judgement ever points to the far goal
Whereto she leads all lives with sure control,
Shaping the hour to suit with distant days.

Enter AGEMEMNON, *in a chariot, with* CASSANDRA *beside him*

LEADER OF CHO. King of Argos and scion of Atreus, de-
      stroyer of Ilios' town,
With what words shall I greet thee aright, how award thee
      they meed of renown,
Neither shortening thy merits unduly, nor aimlessly rush-
      ing beyond?
Our race oft transgresseth in judgement. Too many weak
      mortals are fond
Of the seeming of right, not regarding how Justice offended
      may frown.
Men are ready with sighs for the fall of a friend, while the
      heart is unwrung;
And with smiles for success, where the face is compelled to
      accord with the tongue.
But the shepherd who tells o'er his flock with due heed can-
      not fail to discern
The eyes that in waterish kindness pretend with affection to
      burn.

Then know, for I will not dissemble, when once thou didst
      marshal the host

Thou hadst levied to fight for fair Helen, providing at in-
        finite cost
Forced courage in soldierly bosoms of thousands prepared to
        be slain,
Unlovely to me looked thine image, unskilful thy hand to
        maintain
Thy spirit's true course, as thy bark on that weltering ocean
        was tossed.
But now from my soul's depth arises a voice of warm wel-
        come for those
Whose labour, of doubtful beginning, is fortunate here at
        the close
And in time thou shalt clearly discover, of all thou didst
        leave in command,
Who have failed or been faithful in keeping their charge
        and protecting the land.

AGAM.   Argos, dear country, and my country's gods!
Ye claim my foremost word. Without your aid
I had ne'er returned, nor wrought on Priam's town
This righteous retribution. Yea, the gods,
Moved by the unspoken pleadings, one and all
Gave sentence for the slaughterous sack of Troy.
The blood-stained Vase had all the votes. I' the other
'Hope lingered,' while no plenishing hand came near.—
Her smoke still shows the desolate city's fall.
'Tis Ruin's altar, whence the dying ashes
Of wealth consumed spout forth voluminous breath.
For this we are bound to recompense the gods
With mindful thank-offerings. Our vengeful snare
Held firm, that none escaped, but glorious Ilium
Was, for a woman's sake, ground into dust
By the apparition of the monstrous birth

That, whilst Orion sank, one autumn night,
Leapt from the Horse in Argive panoply.
A ravening lion, o'er the walls he sprang,
· And lapped rich largess of the blood of princes.
　So far forth I address the gods.　Meanwhile,
I bear in mind your moderate words, and like
The spirit they convey.　Your thoughts are mine.
Few men are born so tempered, as to look
Without some envy on a prosperous friend.
The venom of unkindness, lodged within,
Clings to the heart and doubles all annoy;
While men not only mind their own distress,
But groan at other men's prosperity.
How well I know, and could describe, the friend
In name, the mirror of companionship—
Indeed a mirror, a mere fleeting shade.
Odysseus only, who sailed against his will,
Once yoked with me, was ever staunch and true.
　I say it of one of whom to-day I know not
If he be dead or yet alive.
　　　　　　　　　　　For the rest,
Touching the city and the gods, we will call
Our larger council, and deliberate there
In full assembly, studying to preserve
Whatever in the present state is well;
And where some cure is needed, we will try,
With remedies gently administered,
Though sometimes sharp and painful, to prevent
All dangerous malady.—Now, to my hall,
Where my first greeting shall again be made
To the kind gods, who sent me safely forth,
And bring me home in peace.　May Victory,
Since hither she attends us, here remain!

Re-enter CLYTEMNESTRA

CLY. Ye men of Argos, elders of our state,
I will not shame to tell before your face
My wifely love. The fear of man wears off
With time. My heart instructs me to declare
How, while your sovereign tarried before Troy,
My life was doleful. 'Tis no light distress
To sit at home forlorn, the man away,
Malignant rumours ever in one's ears,
One crying he came; another, he had brought
Dishonour, worse even than his death. Moreover,
Had he as many wounds as loose-tongued Fame
Gave forth, a net had fewer holes than he.
And had he died as often as 'twas said,
A second Geryon, with three bodies, he
Had donned a threefold mantle of earth,—I pass
The abyss of ground beneath him,—in each form
Dying once at least. Vexed by such wild reports,
I had often tied the noose above my head
Which others took perforce from off my neck.
Hence, too, Orestes is not here, our son,
The pledge of both our loves. Nay, marvel not!
Our kind ally and friend, Strophius in Phocis,
Keeps him in ward. 'Twas he admonished me
Of a twofold danger, thine beneath Troy-wall,
And of this Argive realm, lest popular fury
Upset the Council;—as mankind are apt,
When one is down, to trample him the more.
None can suspect a shallow pretext there.
As for my tears, they spouted till the fount
Ran dry, and kept no drop. But on my bed
Mine eyes were worn with watching, early and late,

Grieving because the fires of thy return
Were still unkindled. And amidst my dreams
The gnat's small peremptory tones would wake me,
While seeing more dangers than the time could hold
Assailing thee. But now those weary days
Are over, and I shout, exempt from care,
'Here stands the watch-dog of the fold; the mainstay
That saves the vessel; yea, the lofty pillar
That holds the roof from ground:—an only son
Returning to his father; or, to mariners,
Firm land appearing beyond hope, fair day
Seen after tempest; to the thirsty traveller,
A spring of running water 'mid the sand.
To escape from wretchedness is always joy.'
Such terms of greeting have I for my lord.
Let envy rest aloof, since in the past
We have borne much misery. But now, dear king,
Light from that car, not setting foot on earth,
Thou, that hast trodden down the strength of Troy!
Maidens, why tarry ye, that have command
To pave the floor of his path with cloth of grain?
Let there be made forthwith a purple road,
That, to complete the Day's surprise, great Justice
May lead him to his home.

                        For what remains,
Considerate thought, not giving way to slumber,
Shall order well whate'er the gods decree.

      [*The female attendants prepare to lay the carpet*
  Agam. Daughter of Leda, guardian of my Hall,
Thy welcome, like mine absence, hath been long.
Yet praise that rightly squares with my desert
Must come to me from others. Furthermore,
Do not, I pray thee, like some eastern slave,

Meet me with loud and prostrate courtesies,
Nor with this woman-pleasing luxury
Of purple trappings, pluck down on my path
An eye of envy. To the gods alone
Such tribute should be paid. For mortal man
To trample on rich webs of varied hue
To me is a thing by no means void of fear.
I seek for human honours, not divine.
Fame needs no carpets nor embroidered wefts
Beneath her feet, to sound her note of praise
And modesty is Heaven's best gift. When one
Shall end a happy life in peace and joy,
Then celebrate his glory! By this rule
We still may live and prosper, safe from harm.
    CLY. Come, tell me this, and hide not your true thought.
    AGAM. With mind unaltered I will answer thee.
    CLY. You might have vowed this in some hour of
        peril?
    AGAM. I know it. None better. Prompt is that reply.
    CLY. And what of Priam, were he conqueror now?
    AGAM. He had paved his path with broideries, I believe.
    CLY. Be not too sensitive to vulgar blame.
    AGAM. The people's muttered verdict hath great power.
    CLY. Who is not envied, ne'er will be admired.
    AGAM. Contentiousness in woman is not well.
    CLY. Nay, but 'tis gracious, when a victor yields.
    AGAM. Is this a battle in which you care to win?
    CLY. Come, let me triumph on the taker of Troy!
    AGAM. If you must have it so, let some one loose
The shoe that like a slave supports my tread;
Lest, trampling o'er these royal dyes, some god
Smite me with envious glances from afar.
It awes me not a little thus to plunge

In luxury, walking on webs of price.
[*His slippers are removed*
So, that is settled. But receive, I pray thee,
This stranger-woman kindly. Heaven still smiles
When power is used with gentleness. No mortal
Is willingly a captive, but this maid,
Of countless spoils the flower and crown, was given
To me by the army, and attends me home.
[*He descends, while* CASSANDRA *remains upon the car*
Now, since you have subdued me, I obey,
Thus pacing over purple to my hall.

    CLY. Of purple, 'neath the inexhaustible sea,
Enough remains to garnish many a realm
With precious dye for raiment oft renewed.
We too, my monarch, by the help of Heaven,
Possess our share. No poverty is here!
I had vowed to trample many a gorgeous robe,
Had oracles enjoined it on our house,
In hope of bringing home this glorious head.
Our root was still i' the ground. But now returns
The foliage, that gives shadow from the heat.
Thy coming is our warmth in winter time:
But at the season when Zeus turns the grape
From sour green sap to wine, 'tis shady and cool
I' the palace, while its lord is walking there.
[*He goes in*

Zeus—thou fulfillest all—fulfill my prayer!
And take good heed of all thou doest herein!
[*Exit* CLYTEMNESTRA

CHORUS

    What means this haunting Fear
    Incessant hovering near

To scare my prescient heart with vague unrest?
This hymn, unhired, unbidden, of bodings drear?
  Why may not Hope renewed
  With bold belief of good
Regain her wonted seat in my dear breast?
Away, dim dreams! Cease from your vain annoy!
The time is past, when on the sandy coast,
Together moored, the ships their beauty lost,
  Ageing, or ere the host
Might reach their haven 'neath the walls of Troy.

  Not by report I learn
  Our hero's home return.
Myself the eye-witness, I beheld him come.
Yet ne'ertheless my spirit doth inly burn,
  And holding firm no more
  Hope's confidence of yore,
Sings without lyre that self-taught strain of doom.
Not idly stir these inward monishings
Within the throbbing heart that beats on thought
Of judgement, with prophetic dreams distraught.
  Yet may they come to nought,
And let my fears be unaccomplished things!

Great health is prone to end in boundless woe.
 Disease weighs hard on the thin partner-wall.
And when that neighbour hath looked in, we know
 The man's full fortune but prepares his fall.
His ship in her fair course with sudden shock
  Strikes on the viewless rock.
Even then, if caution from a timely sling
Some portion of his wealth to the ocean fling,
His vessel, lightened of her fateful load,
Shall save her timbers from the raging flood,

Her fabric shall not founder in the deep.
Heaven's ample gifts with the revolving years
Shall banish hunger with its brood of fears.
Full harvest from rich furrows they shall reap.

But once let blood of man drop to the ground
  Before his time, and darken all the sod,
What spell to call it upward shall be found?
  What leech so wise?   Though he were all but God
Who learned the secret of restoring breath
      To mortals sunk in death,
Zeus put an end to that for evermore.
The bound is set, and none may pass it o'er.
Else ere the tongue could move, the heart should speak
Of the sore burden, that now bids her break,
As, darkly muttering her dim desire,
O'er-fraught with pain, she may not hope to unwind
The ravelled ponderings of her secret mind,
That inly burns as with consuming fire.

Re-enter CLYTEMNESTRA

  CLY. In with thee too, Cassandra! Get thee in!
Since Heaven in mercy hath consigned thee here
To share our household's lustral waters, one
Of many slaves that stand around our hearth.
Come from that carriage. Be not proud. Descend!
Have we not heard, Alcmena's offspring once
Was sold a slave and felt the galling yoke?
But when misfortune brings one to this pass,
'Tis no small boon to serve an ancient house;
Since they who have harvested beyond their hope
Make cruel masters and exceed the bound.
Thou hast such greeting as I use to a slave.

CHO. She hath said and thou hast heard. Her words
    are clear.
And now thou art in the fatal toils, perchance
Thou mayst obey her. But, methinks, thou art loth.
    CLY. Well, if she be not, like the immigrant bird,
Possessor of a strange outlandish tongue,
My words must find their way and move her will.
    CHO. (*to* CASS.) Go with her! What she sayeth is for
    the best.
As things are now. Come down, and leave that car!
    CLY. I have not time to waste out here with her.
By this the victims at our midmost hearth
Stand ready for the slaughter and the fire;—
Rich thank-offerings for mercies long despaired.
Then, if thou wilt obey me, do it with speed.
But if thou wilt not understand nor speak,
Declare it with the gesture of thy race!
    CHO. 'Twould seem she needs a clear interpreter.
Her ways are as of a creature newly caught.
    CLY. Sure she is mad, and follows crazy thoughts,
Who, leaving her own city newly ta'en,
Comes hither, and hath not the sense to pace
In harness, till she foam away in blood
Her spirit upon the bit.
                 I'll not demean myself
By throwing more words away. [*Exit* CLYTEMNESTRA
    CHO.   But I, unhappy one,
Will not be angry, for I feel for thee.
Come, leave that car deserted, yield to Fate,
And prove the unaccustomed yoke. Descend.

    CASS. (*from the car*). Ai, ai! O Apollo! Apollo!
    CHO. Wherefore *that* cry to Phoebus? Not for him

The voice of mourning.

CASS. Ai! Apollo! Apollo!
Ai! Ai! O Apollo!

CHO. Again she summons with that sound of woe
The god whose ears detest it.

CASS. . . . . O my Apollo
Builder! Destroyer!
Builder of Troy! Destroyer of me!
Once more thy heavy hand with ease hath ruined me.

CHO. Hark! She will prophesy of her despair.
A captive, yet she holds the heavenly fire!

CASS. Apollo! Apollo!
Troy-builder! Destroyer of me!
Ha! What is here? What roof? Whither hast thou
brought me?

CHO. The Atridae's palace. If thou know'st it not,
I tell thee plainly; and thou wilt find it true.

CASS. Ah!
Nay, but a hideous den, abhorred of Heaven;
Guilt-stained with strangled lives, with kinsmen's blood;
A place of sprinkled gore, of clotted horror!
Ah! Faugh!

CHO. Her scent is keen, this stranger's! Like a hound
She snuffs for blood. And she will find, I doubt me.

CASS. Yea! There, there! there! Here's evidence enough!
Smell? Nay—I see, I hear them! Little children
Whose throats are cut, still wailing of their murder,
And the roast flesh, a father tasted—swallowed!

CHO. We have heard of thy renown in prophecy.
But yet forbear. There needs no prophet here.

CASS. Ah! what is this? Oh me!
What strange new grief is risen?

A deed of might! She plans it there even now
      Beneath yon roof, a plague
Hard to remove, not to be borne; an act
Of hate for love; and succour bides aloof,
      Far, far away!
    CHO. This p ophecy is dark to me. The last
Was clear. C city rings with that old woe.
    CASS. Wretch! Wilt thou do it? Ah me!
      The lord of thine embrace,
When thou hast bathed him that his bright limbs glow,—
      How shall I tell it? 'Twill come!
'Tis here! She lifts her hand; she launches at him
      Blow following blow.
    CHO. I understand not yet. The oracular word
Blinds with its riddling purport: I am perplexed.

    CASS. What apparition? Oh the pain! What is it?
      Some net of Death and Hell?
Nay, 'tis the snare o' the chamber, th' accessory
O' the murder. Let yon pack that ravins on the race
Howl, 'Out upon the butchery! Stone her! Stone her!'
    CHO. What cry of ban-dogs bid'st thou curse the house?
Thy speech appals me. To my heart runs back
The death-drop, that when life is ebbing fast
From mortal wounds, and his last beam is pale,
Falls with his setting. Oh! how swift is sorrow!
    CASS. What do I see? Ah, keep away the cow
      From the lordly bull! Look, look!
She hath caught him in the garment, smites, and gores him
With that black weapon of hers. He falls, he falls
I' the watery tun, the guileful, fatal cauldron!

    CHO. I would boast of little skill in prophecies;
But I may guess, this raving bodes no good.

Yet when was soothsaying bright?
What sound of cheer have prophets for the world?
Ills are their stock-in-trade; words are their tools.
          With chanted strains of woe
They strike vain terror into mortal mind.

Cass. Woe! for my hapless doom!
       To fill the cup, I tell my own sad tale!
Why hast thou brought me to this place? Oh misery!
To die with thee? What else? To die! to die!

Cho. Thou art distraught, or else possessed. Some god
Bears thee away to sing of thine own doom
       A wild untutored song, like her
The brown sweet nightingale,—once a princess yonder,
Insatiable of wailing, her sad heart
Still set on sorrow, mourning evermore
For Itys, Itys! 'Tis her life. She blooms
With misery.

Cass.   Oh! for a lot like hers!
The clear-voiced maid, to whom kind gods have given
A feathery form and wings! Safe, calm, sweet life!
Mine, to be cleft in twain with two-edged brand.

Cho. Whence this returning trouble of thy soul,
This god-fraught, vain distress, the ill-omened cry
       That peals in terrifying song?
Whence comes thy music, whence thy thrilling lay?
What limits hath thy Heaven-inspired way?
Who set them? Who hath given the evil word
          Wherewith thy breast is stirred?

Cass. Paris, thy wedding hath destroyed thy house,
Yea, and thy sister!—O Scamander-stream!
Our fathers drank of thee, and by thy shore
I grew, I flourished, oh unhappy I!
But now by dark Cocytus and the banks

Of Acheron, my prophecies shall sound.

    CHO. Now speak'st thou plainly. Even a child might
        know;
         And when I hear that word,
Thy plaintive notes strike me with cruel stings
Of pity and wonder for thy life of pain.

    CASS. Troy, thou art fallen, never to rise. Thy woes
No sacrifice abated nor reprieved
Of all my father slew before the towers,
Poor herb-fed victims! Troy is fallen in fire;
And I, on fire, erelong shall fall in blood.

    CHO. That strain agreeth to thy former words.
         Some god of cruel mind
With mighty force impels thee to this dirge,
As if thy life were doomed. The end I know not.

    CASS. No longer, like a newly married girl,
My word shall peep behind a veil, but flashing
With panted vehemence to meet the day,
'Twill dash, against the shores of Light, a sorrow
Of mightier volume.
               I will expound it. Mark me!
No riddling now! Bear witness if ye find me
Keen to discern or agile to pursue
The trail of long-past crime.
                 There bides within
A band of voices,—all in unison,
Yet neither sweet nor tuneful, for their song
Is not of blessing. Ay, a revel-rout,
Ever emboldened with new draughts of blood,
Within these walls, a furious multitude,
Hard to drive forth, keeps haunt, all of one kin.
They cling to the walls: they hymn the primal curse,
Their fatal hymn; then in due course they spurn

A brother's bed, by a hateful brother mounted.
Say, was that shaft well aimed? Or am I proved
No seer,—a forward babbler at the door?
Declare this on your oath: Have I, or not,
Learnt one old secret of this house of sin?

   Cho. How should an oath, the noblest ever sworn,
Prove healing in this case?

                       Howbeit, I marvel,
Reared overseas, thou shouldst portray the state
Of a strange people, as thou hadst heard and seen.

   Cass. Prophet Apollo thus empowered my soul.

   Cho. Was he, although a god, smit with thy love?

   Cass. Time was, I had blushed to utter such a word.

   Cho. Well-being is daintier than adversity.

   Cass. Sweet was it when he wrestled for my heart.

   Cho. Came ye to close embraces, as men use?

   Cass. I promised Phoebus, but belied my troth.

   Cho. When fired already by the Spirit Divine?

   Cass. Already I foretold my country's woe.

   Cho. How couldst thou 'scape the wrath of Phoebus,
        then?

   Cass. No man believed me from that fatal hour.

   Cho. To us, methinks, thy words seem true.

   Cass.   Oh! oh!
Alas! my misery!
Again the terrible whirlwind comes! the pain
Of truth's deliverance, troubling all within me.

See! the beginning of sorrows! What are these
What dreamlike forms kneel on yon roof? Young boys,
As they'd been slain by those who should have loved them,
Holding a burden piteous to be borne,
Gobbets of flesh, their very own, their entrails,

Clearly discernible,—the heart, the liver,
Of which their father ate!
                            For this, I say,
Vengeance is plotted by a craven lion
That tumbled in the lordly monarch's lair
In his absence,—so kept house for *him*,—alas!
My master. Once a captive, one must bear it!
He ruled the fleet, and razed the towers of Ilium,
But knows not what the monster-woman dares;
What sequel to her garrulous speech and face
Of welcome, brightening as the moon,—like Atè
Lurking in night,—she'll work with wicked speed.
The man-slaying woman! To what horrid form
Shall I compare her, and be true? To Scylla,
That raging mother of death, dwelling in rocks,
Now rending the poor mariner, but once
A pitiless curse to her own?—or Amphisbaena?

Heard ye her triumph? Even as warriors shout
Who turn the battle, so the woman cried,
Seeming to joy in his return from war.

Ye are still incredulous. It makes no difference.
What is to come, will come,—and soon. Thou, seeing,
Shalt pity, and say, 'Her soothsaying was too true!'
    CHO. Thyestes' banquet of his children's flesh
I understood, and shuddered. Fear possessed me
To hear it truly given, each point observed.
But as I listened further, I was lost.
    CASS. Agamemnon's death, I tell thee, thou shalt see.
    CHO. Unhappy one! Speak no ill-omened word!
    CASS. *This* time I summon not the god of healing!
    CHO. Death has no healer. But be it far, I pray!

Cass. Ye pray, while others slay; or are about it.
Cho. What man can be the author of this woe?
Cass. What *man?* Far wide indeed that arrow flew!
Cho. Yea, for I cannot guess who is to do it.
Cass. And yet I have learnt too well the speech of Hellas.
Cho. So hath the Pythoness. Yet her words are dark.
Cass. Oh pain! What burning fire! It comes, it comes!
Lykian Apollo! Woe! me miserable!

This human lioness, couching with a wolf
While the noble lion was away, will kill
Me the unfortunate, a fair prize, to make
One more ingredient in her chalice of bane.
Sharpening her husband's death-knife, she declares
My death, too, shall requite his bringing me.
—Why wear I still these mockeries of my soul,
This wand, these fillets round my neck? I tear ye
Thus! Go to your destruction ere I die!
To pieces with you! Lead the way! I follow!
Enrich some other life with misery!
See! see! Apollo! he is stripping from me
This prophet-mantle.
                    Ay, thou didst visit me
Thine eye beheld me, even in these hallowed weeds,
Insulted, spurned, with those who loved me well.
By our enemies who swept in like a flood.
They called me beggar-priestess, roving seer;
I bore it,—dying with hunger, poor, dismayed!
And now the Seër of seers, Prophet supreme,
Disrobing here his prophetess, conducts me
To this dark ending. For my father's altar,
What waits me now? The block, the bloody knife,
The hot last blow that ends the sacrifice.

Yet shall we die not unobserved of Heaven.
He lives, who shall avenge us. Come he shall,
The mother-slaying scion of his race,
Redeemer of his sire's renown. From far.
The wanderer shall return, and put the cope
On these home troubles. For the gods in Heaven
Have sworn a mighty oath, his father's fall
Shall draw him from his alien dwelling-place.
Why do I linger thus and mourn, since first
I saw my city's ruin; and again
Her captor, judged of the gods, receives this doom?
I will go forward! I will dare to die!
Hail, then thou gate of Hell!

But first, one prayer!
Oh, grant me, all ye gods! a mortal wound!
That with no struggling, while the deathful stream
Flows painlessly away, these eyes may close!

CHO. Deep-thoughted, deeply suffering maid, thy words
Have far extended. If thou know'st thy doom
For certain, how canst thou, like god-driven victim,
Walk boldly toward the altar of thy death?

CASS. It may not be avoided. 'Tis the hour!

CHO. But every moment's respite has some worth.

CASS. The time is come. Small gain were flight to me.

CHO. A bold heart hast thou for thy bitter woe.

CASS. None but the wretched hear such benison.

CHO. Yet mortal life is graced by a noble death.

CASS. Woe for thee, father, and thy noble sons!

[*She is approaching the palace-gate—then turns away*

CHO. What terror turns thee backward from the gate?

CASS. Ah woe!

CHO. What's thine abhorrence? or why criest thou
        thus?

CASS.   These halls exhale with murder! drip with death!
CHO.   'Tis but the reek of household sacrifice.
CASS.   'Tis like a charnel-room.   It steams with gore.
CHO.   Other than Syrian perfume find'st thou, then?
CASS.   Nay, I will go within, and there bewail
Agamemnon's fate and mine.   I have done with life!
Oh strangers! friends!
I shrink not idly, like some timorous bird
Before a bush!   Bear record in that day
When I am dead, and for this woman slain
A woman's life is taken, and, for the man
Whose wife was naught, a man shall meet his doom.
Ye hear my last request before I die.
CHO.   Poor maid!   We pity thy prophetic fall.
CASS.   Once more I would speak, not now with tears, but
          firmly,
Touching myself.   To thee, O Sun, I pray,
Looking my last on thee, that when the Hour
Is here, and vengeance tarries not, I, too,
A captive prey,—soon quelled,—may be avenged.   [*Exit*
CHO.   Ah!   What is mortal life?   When prosperous,
A shadow can o'erturn it, and, when fallen,
A throw o' the wet sponge blurs the picture out.
This is more piteous than the ruin of pride.

Who hath e'er been content with his triumph, or spoken
          to Fortune this word,
—While men point with the finger of envy at halls he hath
          reared for his pride,—
     ' 'Tis enough!   Come not hither again!'
To this king the immortals have given to vanquish the glory
          of Troy,

And, favoured of Heaven, with honour he comes from the
    war to his home.
But if now to requite ancient murders he die in the midst
    of his joy,
      Who shall boast to be free from disaster?

    Agam. (*within*) Ah! Ah! I am mortally stricken
      here, in the palace!

    Cho. 1. Hush! who cries that he is wounded, stricken
      with a mortal stroke?

    Agam. Oh me! Again I am smitten, to the death!

    Cho. 1. It was the king. That groan concluded all.
'Tis finished! Let us join safe counsels here.

    Cho. 2. Then, hear my judgement. Sound we an alarm,
And draw the city to the palace-gate!

    Cho. 3. Nay, let us break within immediately,
And prove the fact before the knife be cold.

    Cho. 4. That likes me better. Let us act, say I,
In some way. 'Tis no time for long debate.

    Cho. 5. One may see plainly, when such signs appear,
Treason and tyranny are near at hand.

    Cho. 6. Ay, we lose time, whilst others are in act
And triumph o'er our solemn feebleness.

    Cho. 7. I know not what to say. To advise is hard,
Since counsel is forestalled by action here.

    Cho. 8. Hard, say you! So think I! 'Twere hard, I
      trow,
With reasoned words to raise the dead to life.

    Cho. 9. Then must we all our days be over-awed
To their subjection who have stained the throne?

    Cho. 10. To die were more endurable than so.
Death is a milder doom than tyranny.

    Cho. 11. Are we diviners, to conclude from groans
He, that so cried, fell with a mortal stroke?

CHO. 12. Let's talk no more of this until we know.
Barren conjecture is a treacherous guide.
    LEADER OF CHO. The sum of all your counsels, then, is
        this:
That we make certain how it goes with the king.
    [*They are approaching the gate, when* CLYTEMNESTRA
        is discovered with the dead body of AGAMEMNON
        enveloped in the embroidered web
    CLY. I, who spake much before to serve my need,
Will here unspeak it,—unappalled by shame.
How else prepare the hostile net to slay
One's foe, supposed one's friend, and fence it high
Beyond o'erleaping?—Time, and thought still brooding
On that old quarrel, brought me to this blow.
'Tis done, and here I stand: here where I smote him!—
I so contrived it,—that I'll ne'er deny,—
As neither loophole nor defence was left him.
I had set round, like a stake-net for fish,
A labyrinth of hangings, with no outlet,
A limb-embarrassing wealth of woven folds.
I smote him, twice: and with the second groan
He sank: and when he had fallen, I gave a third
Last stroke, to crown the sacrifice, and grace
Pluto, preserver of the dead. Even then,
His soul on wing for Hades, his keen breath
Smote me with drops of slaughter, whose dark dew
Refreshed my spirit, even as the bladed corn
That swells to the ear, delighteth in Heaven's rain.
Such—oh ye Argive elders who stand here,—
Such is the fact. Whereat, an if ye will,
Rejoice ye! Howsoe'er, it is my boast.
Yea, were libation meet o'er human victim,

Here 'twere most righteous. Such a cup of death
He filled with household crime, and now, returning,
Has drained in retribution.
    Cho.   Wondrous bold
Of tongue art thou, to boast thus o'er thy lord!
    Cly. Presume ye, as though my thoughts were woman-
        ish?
I dare your wisdoms. Ye know all, and—blame me
Or praise,—'tis one to me. This corpse, I tell you,
Is Agamemnon, once my lord;—his death
    The work of this right hand, proud to have wrought
A masterpiece so righteous. Ay, 'tis true.
    Cho.   Woman, what evil food
    From either element, of earth or sea,
      Solid or liquid, mingling with thy blood
          Hath prompted thee
      To kill such sacrifice, and then
        Fling back from thee the muttered curse of men?
Hast thou cut him off? Thou shalt be cut off from the
        state;
      Our citizens shall hate thee with firm hate.
    Cly. That is your sentence. I must fly the land
With public execration on my head.
Wise justicers! what said ye, then, to him
Who slew his child, nor recked of her dear blood
More than if sacrificing some ewe-lamb
From countless flocks that choked the teeming fold,
But slew the priceless travail of my womb
For a charm, to allay the wind from Thrace? How say
      you?
Should he not have been banished by your voice
To purge the state? Yet, hearing of my deed,

Ye are swift and harsh in judgement.

Threaten, then,
Even as ye list; but so as, being assured,
That force must win the day. If so ye win,
I yield. But if Zeus give my plans success,—
And they are deeply laid,—you shall be taught,
Old as ye are to learn, the path of peace.

CHO. Haughty thy spirit, and proud
Thy vaunting. But as thine infatuate soul
Inflamed with murder, in defiance loud
   Contemns control,
  While lurid light is in thine eye,
 Intoxicate with impious butchery,—
Unavenged, with no lover at hand, in thy Destiny's day,
  With blow for blow the forfeit thou shalt pay.

CLY. Say you? Then hear mine oath. By mighty Justice,
Final avenger of my murdered child,
By Atè and Erinys, gods of power,
To whom I sacrificed this man, I look not
For danger as an inmate, whiles our hearth
Is lightened by Aegisthus, evermore,
As hitherto, constant in love to me;
My shield, my courage! He is fallen, who shamed me
In dalliance with Chryséis and the rest
Before the Trojan wall. Ay, and that other,
His prophet-mistress, his oracular love,
His captive-conqueress, that shared his bed
On shore, his bench i' the ship:—she too now lies
In death. They have full recompense. You see
His fortune—as for her, she tuned her lay
Most swanlike for her end, wailing their doom.
So died the damsel this man brought to lend

New savour to the softness of my bed.

   CHO. O for some speedy stroke,
Not of sharp agony nor lingering pain,
To bring on us the unawakening sleep!
Since he, our gentlest guardian, is subdued,
And through a woman's guilt.—A woman slew him!
Infatuate Helen, who alone didst send
So many souls to Hades before Troy!
A life worth all the rest thy sister's deed
Hath quenched in darkness. From one little seed
Is grown a strong and ever-spreading tree
Of man-destroying strife and misery.

   CLY. Pray not for your death, overburdened with what
          hath been done;
Neither turn your displeasure on Helen, of Hellas the bane,
Who sped many souls to destruction and caused unendur-
          able pain!

   CHO. O demon of the home,
That with alternate violence doth fall
On either branch of Pelops' ancient line,
Thou to my bitter sorrow wieldest here
Man-braving boldness in a woman's mind.
Like hateful raven, o'er her husband's corse
She stands and croaks at us, in accents hoarse,
Her proudly inharmonious funeral hymn.

.   .   .   .

   CLY. At length there is truth on your lips. Ye name
          rightly the Fiend overgrown
   Whose seed in this mansion was sown.
'Tis of him that the blood-lapping lust at its core hath been
          nursed.

Ere the grief from old wounds hath abated, fresh fountains
    of bloodshed are burst.
  Cho. Mighty and fell of wrath
Declar'st thou then the Genius of the race;
Recalling a disastrous history
Of dire offences irremediable
And endless. Zeus the cause;—for what in man
Eludes the author of the Eternal Plan?
      Oh king, my king, how shall I weep for thee?
      What words of affection shall flow from my heart?
Thou art there in that web of the spider, dishonoured in
    death,
      Oh horror! oh murderous guile!
      Dishonoured, and cleft with the sword,
      The warm life yet running from thee!
  Cly. Ye proclaim it my deed. Yet beware!
      Say not I was wife to the king.
  'Tis the spirit of Vengeance awaking from sleep
For the banquet by Atreus of old to Thyestes cruelly given,
Putting on the resemblance of her that was queen to the
    dead,
    That hath visited all upon him,
And hath sternly repaid a grown victim for little ones
    slain.
  Cho. That this is not thy work
Who will bear witness? The offence is thine,
Whatever spirit of hoarded recompense
From elder ages may have wrought with thee.
Not yet accomplished is the course of strife,
The clotted guilt of infant gore yet cries
For kindred streams of bloody sacrifice,
All from one source, life rendered still for life.
      Oh king, my king, how shall I weep for thee?

What words of affection shall flow from my heart?
Thou art there in that web of the spider, dishonoured in
 death,
  Oh horror! oh murderous guile!
  Dishonoured, and cleft with the sword,
  The warm life yet running from thee!
 CLY. Prate not of dishonour! 'Deserving' were rather
  the word.
Had *he* not prepared for his house an encumbrance of woe?
  Let him not loudly plead there below
That in paying the price of her death whom a nation de-
 plored,
The branch I had reared from his loins, he is slain with
  iniquitous sword.
  Men shall reap what they sow!
 CHO. I am baffled and amazed, and know not whither
To turn me now the house begins to totter
Lashed with red rain, that saps it to the fall.
I fear it! This is no mere drizzling shower.
Fate now is whetting Justice' heavy sword
On a new whetstone, for fresh deeds of harm.

O Earth, Earth! would thou hadst covered me,
 Ere I saw in his low-lying bed,
'Twixt the sides of yon bath-tub of silver, the king whom
 I love!

Who shall bury his corpse, who lament him?
  Wilt *thou* have the heart,
Having slain thine own husband, to peal forth his dirge
And atone with light breath for the heavy offence thou
 hast done?
Ah, who shall be found to repeat for the man now divine

The due praise o'er his grave, pouring tears with each word
    sorely wrung
  By deep thought from the truth of his soul?
CLY. Have no care. 'Tis not yours to provide. I will
    bury the man whom I slew.
No train from the palace shall wail round his bier. But
    his daughter, to yield him his due,
Running forward to welcome her sire at the quickly passed
    ford of the dead,—
His Iphianassa,—shall open her arms and shall cling,
  With a kiss, to the king!
CHO. Reproaches cross. The battle is hard to judge.
Robber is robbed, slayer slain. Revenge is sure.
Firm stands, while Zeus remains upon his throne,
One law, 'Who doeth shall suffer.' Who may cast
The brood of curses from yon roof? The race
Is joined and welded to calamity.
CLY. Therein thou hast prophesied aright. But I
Here make my compact with the hellish Power
That haunts the house of Atreus. What has been,
Though hard, we will endure. But let him leave
This roof, and plague some other race henceforth
With kindred-harrowing strife. Small share of wealth
Shall amply serve, now I have made an end
Of mutual-murdering madness in this hall.

Enter AEGISTHUS

AEG. Sweet day of recompense, I hail thy light!
Now, lords of yon wide heaven, I recognize
Your jurisdiction o'er the griefs of men,
When I behold this man, to my great joy,
Laid in yon shroud of the Erinyes,
So punished for his father's act of guile.

Atreus his father, ruling the Argive land,
But challenged of his right, to tell it plainly,
By his own brother and my sire, Thyestes,
Drave him an exile from his country and home.
Then poor Thyestes, coming back to Argos
A humble suppliant at his brother's hearth,
Obtained remission of the doom of death.
And Atreus, feigning gladness that these fields
Should not be darkened with fraternal blood,
Received him at a banquet, with great show,
But little heart, of hospitality.
As holding a high day of sacrifice,
He set before him—his own children's flesh.
The feet and hands with tell-tale finger-tips
He kept concealed where by himself he sate
At head o' the board: and with those marks away
My father knew not, but received and ate
What brought unbounded sorrow, as thou seëst,
To all our race. For when he came to know
The horror that was brought, sickening he fell
Back from that carnage with a cry, and laid
This dreadful curse on the Pelopidae,
That as he kicked the banquet to the ground,
All Pelops' line might have like overthrow.
Hence came *his* fall you now behold.

And I
Have the best right to have contrived his death.
I, my poor father's thirteenth child, was driven
Along with him, a babe in swaddling bands.
Now, Justice brings me home, a man indeed.
And while still out of doors I laid my hand
On this mine enemy, with plans secure
Weaving the plot that should entangle him

So that to-day I were not loth to die,
Seeing him fast in Retribution's net.

CHO. Aegisthus, to insult over the fallen
Wins not my homage. You confess to have slain
Agamemnon by your will; alone to have planned
This piteous massacre! The people's curse
Awaits thee, be thou sure, with stones to boot.

AEG. Thou say'st it! thou, that pliest the nether oar,
While those on the top-bench manage the spear!
Thine age shall find how hard a lesson 'tis
When old men have to learn obedience.
Bondage and prison-fare combined with eld
Work miracles in healing froward spirits.
Behold the proverb here exemplified:—
'Kick not at goad-pricks, else your heels shall rue!'

CHO. (*to* CLY.) Woman, and when the king returned
          from war,
Hadst thou, that kept his house, shaming moreover
Thy husband's bed, prepared for him this death?

          [CLYTEMNESTRA *remains silent*

AEG. Again your tongue leads you the way to woe!
The opposite of Orpheus' voice is thine.
He drew all after him with charming lay,
But thou, with foolish clamour rousing wrath,
Shalt be dragged off, that power may humble thee.

CHO. Methinks I see thee lord of Argive men!
That, when thou hadst devised this massacre,
Too craven wert thyself to strike the blow.

AEG. Guile was the woman's function. I, moreover,
Had waked suspicion from our ancient feud.—
His wealth is mine to use, and I will use it
To rule your city. He that disobeys
Shall be bowed down beneath my heavy yoke,

No minion of the side-trace and the stall!
Darkness and hunger, grooming him together,
In harsh consent shall join to make him tame.

   Cho. Thou didst not quell him, coward that thou wert,
Thou durst not cope with him; a woman slew him,
Staining our country and our country's gods!
O that Orestes, if he lives to-day,
Might yet return auspiciously to Argos,
And kill both tyrants in his prime of power!

   Aeg. So, ye choose that line of talk and conduct! Ye
       shall quickly find——
Ho, brave guards, come rally round me! Here's a field-day
       to your mind.

   Cho. Come, let every man make ready for the encounter,
       sword in hand!

   Aeg. Come, I dare the death in combat for mine empire
       o'er the land.

   Cho. 'Death!' that word is right: I embrace it. Fortune,
       let the omen stand!

   Cly. Dearest one, let strife have ending. Add not to
       the heap of ill:
As it is, of troublous labour we are doomed to reap our fill.
Woes enow are here already; let not blood o'erpass the
       bound.
Back, ye dotards; know your places! Run in your ap-
       pointed round,
Lest ye rue the deeds ye ponder; let your rude contention
       cease!

Might but this be all of sorrow, we would bargain now
       for peace,
Harassed by the heavy heel of God that trampled on our
       lot.

So resolves my woman's wisdom, whether men give heed
or not.

AEG.   Can I hear that these should idly from submission
break away,

Flaunting proud rebellious phrases in defiance of my sway,

Holding light the Power that guides us as our Providence
to-day?

CHO.   Men of Argos ne'er will cringe in homage to a
man of crime.

AEG.   You shall yet repeat that language, visited in after-
time.

CHO.   Not if God direct Orestes homeward for his
people's good.

AEG.   Well I know that men in exile make of Hope their
daily food.

CHO.   Do thy worst! Grow fat, polluting Justice. It is
now thine hour.

AEG.   Know that one day for this folly thou shalt answer to my power.

CHO.   Boast thee without fear exulting, like a cock beside
the hen!

CLY.   Care not for the idle yelpings of these old and
feeble men.

I and thou together ruling with a firm and even hand

Will control and keep in order both the palace and the
land.

OEDIPUS THE KING

BY

SOPHOCLES

DRAMATIS PERSONÆ

Oedipus.
The Priest of Zeus.
Creon.
Chorus of Theban Elders.
Teiresias.
Jocasta.
Messenger.
Herd of Laius.
Second Messenger.

Scene:—Thebes. Before the Palace of Oedipus.

ARGUMENT

To Laïus, King of Thebes, an oracle foretold that the child born to him by his queen Jocasta would slay his father and wed his mother. So when in time a son was born the infant's feet were riveted together and he was left to die on Mount Cithaeron. But a shepherd found the babe and tended him, and delivered him to another shepherd who took him to his master, the King of Corinth. Polybus being childless adopted the boy, who grew up believing that he was indeed the King's son. Afterwards doubting his parentage he inquired of the Delphic god and heard himself the weird declared before to Laïus. Wherefore he fled from what he deemed his father's house and in his flight he encountered and unwittingly slew his father Laïus. Arriving at Thebes he answered the riddle of the Sphinx and the grateful Thebans made their deliverer king. So he reigned in the room of Laïus, and espoused the widowed queen. Children were born to them and Thebes prospered under his rule, but again a grievous plague fell upon the city. Again the oracle was consulted and it bade them purge themselves of blood-guiltiness. Oedipus denounces the crime of which he is unaware, and undertakes to track out the criminal. Step by step it is brought home to him that he is the man. The closing scene reveals Jocasta slain by her own hand and Oedipus blinded by his own act and praying for death or exile.

OEDIPUS THE KING

*Suppliants of all ages are seated round the altar at the
palace doors, at their head a* PRIEST OF ZEUS.
To them enter OEDIPUS.

OEDIPUS

My children, latest born to Cadmus old,
Why sit ye here as suppliants, in your hands
Branches of olive filleted with wool?
What means this reek of incense everywhere,
And everywhere laments and litanies?
Children, it were not meet that I should learn
From others, and am hither come, myself,
I Oedipus, your world-renownèd king.
Ho! aged sire, whose venerable locks
Proclaim thee spokesman of this company,
Explain your mood and purport. Is it dread
Of ill that moves you or a boon ye crave?
My zeal in your behalf ye cannot doubt;
Ruthless indeed were I and obdurate
If such petitioners as you I spurned.

PRIEST

Yea, Oedipus, my sovereign lord and king,
Thou seest how both extremes of age besiege
Thy palace altars—fledglings hardly winged,
And greybeards bowed with years; priests, as am I
Of Zeus, and these the flower of our youth.
Meanwhile, the common folk, with wreathèd boughs

Crowd our two market-places, or before
Both shrines of Pallas congregate, or where
Ismenus gives his oracles by fire.
For, as thou seest thyself, our ship of State,
Sore buffeted, can no more lift her head,
Foundered beneath a weltering surge of blood.
A blight is on our harvest in the ear,
A blight upon the grazing flocks and herds,
A blight on wives in travail; and withal
Armed with his blazing torch the God of Plague
Hath swooped upon our city emptying
The house of Cadmus, and the murky realm
Of Pluto is full fed with groans and tears.
　　Therefore, O King, here at thy hearth we sit,
I and these children; not as deeming thee
A new divinity, but the first of men;
First in the common accidents of life,
And first in visitations of the Gods.
Art thou not he who coming to the town
Of Cadmus freed us from the tax we paid
To the fell songstress?　Nor hadst thou received
Prompting from us or been by others schooled;
No, by a god inspired (so all men deem,
And testify) didst thou renew our life.
And now, O Oedipus, our peerless king,
All we thy votaries beseech thee, find
Some succour, whether by a voice from heaven
Whispered, or haply known by human wit.
Tried counsellors, methinks, are aptest found [1]
To furnish for the future pregnant rede.
Upraise, O chief of men, upraise our State!

---

[1] Dr. Kennedy and others render "Since to men of experience I
see that also comparisons of their counsels are in most lively use."

Look to thy laurels! for thy zeal of yore
Our country's saviour thou art justly hailed:
O never may we thus record thy reign:—
"He raised us up only to cast us down."
Uplift us, build our city on a rock.
Thy happy star ascendant brought us luck,
O let it not decline! If thou wouldst rule
This land, as now thou reignest, better sure
To rule a peopled than a desert realm.
Nor battlements nor galleys aught avail,
If men to man and guards to guard them fail.

OEDIPUS

Ah! my poor children, known, ah, known too well,
The quest that brings you hither and your need.
Ye sicken all, well wot I, yet my pain,
How great soever yours, outtops it all.
Your sorrow touches each man severally,
Him and none other, but I grieve at once
Both for the general and myself and you.
Therefore ye rouse no sluggard from day-dreams.
Many, my children, are the tears I've wept,
And threaded many a maze of weary thought.
Thus pondering one clue of hope I caught,
And tracked it up; I have sent Menoeceus' son,
Creon, my consort's brother, to inquire
Of Pythian Phoebus at his Delphic shrine,
How I might save the State by act or word.
And now I reckon up the tale of days
Since he set forth, and marvel how he fares.
'Tis strange, this endless tarrying, passing strange.
But when he comes, then I were base indeed,
If I perform not all the god declares.

PRIEST

Thy words are well timed; even as thou speakest
That shouting tells me Creon is at hand.

OEDIPUS

O King Apollo! may his joyous looks
Be presage of the joyous news he brings!

PRIEST

As I surmise, 'tis welcome; else his head
Had scarce been crowned with berry-laden bays.

OEDIPUS

We soon shall know; he's now in earshot range.
Enter CREON
My royal cousin, say, Menoeceus' child,
What message hast thou brought us from the god?

CREON

Good news, for e'en intolerable ills,
Finding right issue, tend to naught but good.

OEDIPUS

How runs the oracle? thus far thy words
Give me no ground for confidence or fear.

CREON

If thou wouldst hear my message publicly,
I'll tell thee straight, or with thee pass within.

OEDIPUS

Speak before all; the burden that I bear
Is more for these my subjects than myself.

CREON

Let me report then all the god declared.
King Phoebus bids us straitly extirpate
A fell pollution that infests the land,
And no more harbour an inveterate sore.

OEDIPUS

What expiation means he? What's amiss?

CREON

Banishment, or the shedding blood for blood.
This stain of blood makes shipwreck of our state.

OEDIPUS

Whom can he mean the miscreant thus denounced?

CREON

Before thou didst assume the helm of State,
The sovereign of this land was Laïus.

OEDIPUS

I heard as much, but never saw the man.

CREON

He fell; and now the god's command is plain:
Punish his takers-off, whoe'er they be.

OEDIPUS

Where are they? Where in the wide world to find
The far, faint traces of a bygone crime?

CREON

In this land, said the god; "who seeks shall find;
Who sits with folded hands or sleeps is blind."

OEDIPUS

Was he within his palace, or afield,
Or travelling, when Laïus met his fate?

CREON

Abroad; he started, so he told us, bound
For Delphi, but he never thence returned.

OEDIPUS

Came there no news, no fellow-traveller
To give some clue that might be followed up?

CREON

But one escaped, who flying for dear life,
Could tell of all he saw but one thing sure.

OEDIPUS

And what was that? One clue might lead us far,
With but a spark of hope to guide our quest.

CREON

Robbers, he told us, not one bandit but
A troop of knaves, attacked and murdered him.

OEDIPUS

Did any bandit dare so bold a stroke,
Unless indeed he were suborned from Thebes?

CREON

So 'twas surmised, but none was found to avenge
His murder mid the trouble that ensued.

OEDIPUS

What trouble can have hindered a full quest,
When royalty had fallen thus miserably?

CREON

The riddling Sphinx compelled us to let slide
The dim past and attend to instant needs.

OEDIPUS

Well, *I* will start afresh and once again
Make dark things clear. Right worthy the concern
Of Phoebus, worthy thine too, for the dead;
I also, as is meet, will lend my aid
To avenge this wrong to Thebes and to the god.
Not for some far-off kinsman, but myself,
Shall I expel this poison in the blood;
For whoso slew that king might have a mind
To strike me too with his assassin hand.
Therefore in righting him I serve myself.
Up, children, haste ye, quit these altar stairs,
Take hence your suppliant wands, go summon hither
The Theban commons. With the god's good help
Success is sure; 'tis ruin if we fail.

[*Exeunt* OEDIPUS *and* CREON

PRIEST

Come, children, let us hence; these gracious words
Forestall the very purpose of our suit.
And may the god who sent this oracle
Save us withal and rid us of this pest.

[*Exeunt* PRIEST *and* SUPPLIANTS

CHORUS

Sweet-voiced daughter of Zeus from thy gold-paved Pythian
    shrine
        Wafted to Thebes divine,
What dost thou bring me? My soul is racked and shivers
    with fear.
        (Healer of Delos, hear!)
Hast thou some pain unknown before,
Or with the circling years renewest a penance of yore?
Offspring of golden Hope, thou voice immortal, O tell me.

First on Athenè I call; O Zeus-born goddess, defend!
        Goddess and sister, befriend,
Artemis, Lady of Thebes, high-throned in the midst of our
    mart!
        Lord of the death-winged dart!
        Your threefold aid I crave
    From death and ruin our city to save.
If in the days of old when we nigh had perished, ye drave
From our land the fiery plague, be near us now and de-
    fend us!

    Ah me, what countless woes are mine!
    All our host is in decline;
    Weaponless my spirit lies.
    Earth her gracious fruits denies;
    Women wail in barren throes;
    Life on life downstricken goes,
    Swifter than the wild bird's flight,
    Swifter than the Fire-God's might,
    To the westering shores of Night.

    Wasted thus by death on death
    All our city perisheth,

Corpses spread infection round;
None to tend or mourn is found.
Wailing on the altar stair
Wives and grandams rend the air—
Long-drawn moans and piercing cries
Blent with prayers and litanies.
Golden child of Zeus, O hear
Let thine angel face appear!

And grant that Ares whose hot breath I feel,
    Though without targe or steel
He stalks, whose voice is as the battle shout,
    May turn in sudden rout,
To the unharboured Thracian waters sped,
    Or Amphitritè's bed.
    For what night leaves undone,
    Smit by the morrow's sun
Perisheth. Father Zeus, whose hand
Doth wield the lightning brand,
Slay him beneath thy levin bolt, we pray,
    Slay him, O slay!
O that thine arrows too, Lycean King,
    From the taut bow's gold string,
Might fly abroad, the champions of our rights;
    Yea, and the flashing lights
Of Artemis, wherewith the huntress sweeps
    Across the Lycian steeps.
Thee too I call with golden-snooded hair,
    Whose name our land doth bear,
Bacchus to whom thy Maenads Evoe shout;
    Come with thy bright torch, rout,
      Blithe god whom we adore,
      The god whom gods abhor.

Enter OEDIPUS

OEDIPUS

Ye pray; 'tis well, but would ye hear my words
And heed them and apply the remedy,
Ye might perchance find comfort and relief.
Mind you, I speak as one who comes a stranger
To this report, no less than to the crime;
For how unaided could I track it far
Without a clue? Which lacking (for too late
Was I enrolled a citizen of Thebes)
This proclamation I address to all:—
Thebans, if any knows the man by whom
Laïus, son of Labdacus, was slain,
I summon him to make clean shrift to me.
And if he shrinks, let him reflect that thus
Confessing he shall 'scape the capital charge;
For the worst penalty that shall befall him
Is banishment—unscathed he shall depart.
But if an alien from a foreign land
Be known to any as the murderer,
Let him who knows speak out, and he shall have
Due recompense from me and thanks to boot.
But if ye still keep silence, if through fear
For self or friends ye disregard my hest,
Hear what I then resolve: I lay my ban
On the assassin whosoe'er he be.
Let no man in this land, whereof I hold
The sovereign rule, harbour or speak to him;
Give him no part in prayer or sacrifice
Or lustral rites, but hound him from your homes.
For this is our defilement, so the god
Hath lately shewn to me by oracles.
Thus as their champion I maintain the cause

Both of the god and of the murdered King.
And on the murderer this curse I lay
(On him and all the partners in his guilt):—
Wretch, may he pine in utter wretchedness!
And for myself, if with my privity
He gain admittance to my hearth, I pray
The curse I laid on others fall on me.
See that ye give effect to all my hest,
For my sake and the god's and for our land,
A desert blasted by the wrath of heaven.
For, let alone the god's express command,
It were a scandal ye should leave unpurged
The murder of a great man and your king,
Nor track it home. And now that I am lord,
Successor to his throne, his bed, his wife,
(And had he not been frustrate in the hope
Of issue, common children of one womb
Had forged a closer bond twixt him and me,
But Fate swooped down upon him), therefore I
His blood-avenger will maintain his cause
As though he were my sire, and leave no stone
Unturned to track the assassin or avenge
The son of Labdacus, of Polydore,
Of Cadmus, and Agenor first of the race.
And for the disobedient thus I pray:
May the gods send them neither timely fruits
Of earth, nor teeming increase of the womb,
But may they waste and pine, as now they waste,
Aye and worse stricken; but to all of you,
My loyal subjects who approve my acts,
May Justice, our ally, and all the gods
Be gracious and attend you evermore.

CHORUS

The oath thou profferest, sire, I take and swear.
I slew him not myself, nor can I name
The slayer. For the quest, 'twere well, methinks
That Phoebus, who proposed the riddle, himself
Should give the answer—who the murderer was.

OEDIPUS

Well argued; but no living man can hope
To force the gods to speak against their will.

CHORUS

May I then say what seems next best to me?

OEDIPUS

Aye, if there be a third best, tell it too.

CHORUS

My liege, if any man sees eye to eye
With our lord Phoebus, 'tis our prophet, lord
Teiresias; he of all men best might guide
A searcher of this matter to the light.

OEDIPUS

Here too my zeal has nothing lagged, for twice
At Creon's instance have I sent to fetch him,
And long I marvel why he is not here.

CHORUS

I mind me too of rumours long ago—
Mere gossip.

OEDIPUS

Tell them, I would fain know all.

CHORUS

'Twas said he fell by travellers.

OEDIPUS

So I heard,
But none has seen the man who saw him fall.

CHORUS

Well, if he knows what fear is, he will quail
And flee before the terror of thy curse.

OEDIPUS

Words scare not him who blenches not at deeds.

CHORUS

But here is one to arraign him. Lo, at length
They bring the god-inspirèd seer in whom
Above all other men is truth inborn.
Enter TEIRESIAS, *led by a boy.*

OEDIPUS

Teiresias, seer who comprehendest all,
Lore of the wise and hidden mysteries,
High things of heaven and low things of the earth,
Thou knowest, though thy blinded eyes see naught,
What plague infects our city; and we turn
To thee, O seer, our one defence and shield.
The purport of the answer that the God
Returned to us who sought his oracle,

The messengers have doubtless told thee—how
One course alone could rid us of the pest,
To find the murderers of Laïus,
And slay them or expel them from the land.
Therefore begrudging neither augury
Nor other divination that is thine,
O save thyself, thy country, and thy king,
Save all from this defilement of blood shed.
On thee we rest. This is man's highest end,
To others' service all his powers to lend.

TEIRESIAS

Alas, alas, what misery to be wise
When wisdom profits nothing! This old lore
I had forgotten; else I were not here.

OEDIPUS

What ails thee? Why this melancholy mood?

TEIRESIAS

Let me go home; prevent me not; 'twere best
That thou shouldst bear thy burden and I mine.

OEDIPUS

For shame! no true-born Theban patriot
Would thus withhold the word of prophecy.

TEIRESIAS

Thy words, O king, are wide of the mark, and I
For fear lest I too trip like thee . . .

OEDIPUS

                                    Oh speak,
Withhold not, I adjure thee, if thou know'st,
Thy knowledge. We are all thy suppliants.

TEIRESIAS

Aye, for ye all are witless, but my voice
Will ne'er reveal my miseries—or thine.[1]

OEDIPUS

What then, thou knowest, and yet willst not speak!
Wouldst thou betray us and destroy the State?

TEIRESIAS

I will not vex myself nor thee. Why ask
Thus idly what from me thou shalt not learn?

OEDIPUS

Monster! thy silence would incense a flint.
Will nothing loose thy tongue? Can nothing melt thee,
Or shake thy dogged taciturnity?

TEIRESIAS

Thou blam'st my mood and seest not thine own
Wherewith thou art mated; no, thou taxest me.

OEDIPUS

And who could stay his choler when he heard
How insolently thou dost flout the State?

TEIRESIAS

Well, it will come what will, though I be mute.

OEDIPUS

Since come it must, thy duty is to tell me.

[1] Literally "not to call them thine," but the Greek may be rendered "In order not to reveal thine."

TEIRESIAS

I have no more to say; storm as thou willst,
And give the rein to all thy pent-up rage.

OEDIPUS

Yea, I am wroth, and will not stint my words,
But speak my whole mind. Thou methinks art he,
Who planned the crime, aye, and performed it too,
All save the assassination; and if thou
Hadst not been blind, I had been sworn to boot
That thou alone didst do the bloody deed.

TEIRESIAS

Is it so?   Then I charge thee to abide
By thine own proclamation; from this day
Speak not to these or me. Thou art the man,
Thou the accursed polluter of this land.

OEDIPUS

Vile slanderer, thou blurtest forth these taunts,
And think'st forsooth as seer to go scot free.

TEIRESIAS

Yea, I am free, strong in the strength of truth.

OEDIPUS

Who was thy teacher? not methinks thy art.

TEIRESIAS

Thou, goading me against my will to speak.

OEDIPUS

What speech? repeat it and resolve my doubt.

TEIRESIAS

Didst miss my sense or wouldst thou goad me on?

OEDIPUS

I but half caught thy meaning; say it again.

TEIRESIAS

I say thou art the murderer of the man
Whose murderer thou pursuest.

OEDIPUS

Thou shalt rue it
Twice to repeat so gross a calumny.

TEIRESIAS

Must I say more to aggravate thy rage?

OEDIPUS

Say all thou wilt; it will be but waste of breath.

TEIRESIAS

I say thou livest with thy nearest kin
In infamy, unwitting of thy shame.

OEDIPUS

Think'st thou for aye unscathed to wag thy tongue?

TEIRESIAS

Yea, if the might of truth can aught prevail.

OEDIPUS

With other men, but not with thee, for thou
In ear, wit, eye, in everything art blind.

TEIRESIAS

Poor fool to utter gibes at me which all
Here present will cast back on thee ere long.

OEDIPUS

Offspring of endless Night, thou hast no power
O'er me or any man who sees the sun.

TEIRESIAS

No, for thy weird is not to fall by me.
I leave to Apollo what concerns the god.

OEDIPUS

Is this a plot of Creon, or thine own?

TEIRESIAS

Not Creon, thou thyself art thine own bane.

OEDIPUS

O wealth and empiry and skill by skill
Outwitted in the battlefield of life,
What spite and envy follow in your train!
See, for this crown the State conferred on me,
A gift, a thing I sought not, for this crown
The trusty Creon, my familiar friend,
Hath lain in wait to oust me and suborned
This mountebank, this juggling charlatan,
This tricksy beggar-priest, for gain alone
Keen-eyed, but in his proper art stone-blind.
Say, sirrah, hast thou ever proved thyself
A prophet? When the riddling Sphinx was here
Why hadst thou no deliverance for this folk?

And yet the riddle was not to be solved
By guess-work but required the prophet's art;
Wherein thou wast found lacking; neither birds
Nor sign from heaven helped thee, but *I* came,
The simple Oedipus; *I* stopped her mouth
By mother wit, untaught of auguries.
This is the man whom thou wouldst undermine,
In hope to reign with Creon in my stead.
Methinks that thou and thine abettor soon
Will rue your plot to drive the scapegoat out.
Thank thy grey hairs that thou hast still to learn
What chastisement such arrogance deserves.

CHORUS

To us it seems that both the seer and thou,
O Oedipus, have spoken angry words.
This is no time to wrangle but consult
How best we may fulfil the oracle.

Balance

TEIRESIAS

King as thou art, free speech at least is mine
To make reply; in this I am thy peer.
I own no lord but Loxias; him I serve
And ne'er can stand enrolled as Creon's man.
Thus then I answer: since thou hast not spared
To twit me with my blindness—thou hast eyes,
Yet see'st not in what misery thou art fallen,
Nor where thou dwellest nor with whom for mate.
Dost know thy lineage? Nay, thou know'st it not,
And all unwitting art a double foe
To thine own kin, the living and the dead;
Aye and the dogging curse of mother and sire
One day shall drive thee, like a two-edged sword,

Beyond our borders, and the eyes that now
See clear shall see henceforward endless night.
Ah whither shall thy bitter cry not reach,
What crag in all Cithaeron but shall then
Reverberate thy wail, when thou hast found
With what a hymeneal thou wast borne
Home, but to no fair haven, on the gale!
Aye, and a flood of ills thou guessest not
Shall set thyself and children in one line.
Flout then both Creon and my words, for none
Of mortals shall be stricken worse than thou.

OEDIPUS

Must I endure this fellow's insolence?
A murrain on thee! Get thee hence! Begone
Avaunt! and never cross my threshold more.

TEIRESIAS

I ne'er had come hadst thou not bidden me.

OEDIPUS

I knew not thou wouldst utter folly, else
Long hadst thou waited to be summoned here.

TEIRESIAS

Such am I—as it seems to thee a fool.
But to the parents who begat thee, wise.

OEDIPUS

What sayest thou—"parents"? Who begat me, speak?

TEIRESIAS

This day shall be thy birth-day, and thy grave.

OEDIPUS

Thou lov'st to speak in riddles and dark words.

TEIRESIAS

In reading riddles who so skilled as thou?

OEDIPUS

Twit me with that wherein my greatness lies.

TEIRESIAS

And yet this very greatness proved thy bane.

OEDIPUS

No matter if I saved the commonwealth.

TEIRESIAS

'Tis time I left thee. Come, boy, take me home.

OEDIPUS

Aye, take him quickly, for his presence irks
And lets me; gone, thou canst not plague me more.

TEIRESIAS

I go, but first will tell thee why I came.
Thy frown I dread not, for thou canst not harm me.
Hear then: this man whom thou hast sought to arrest
With threats and warrants this long while, the wretch
Who murdered Laïus—that man is here.
He passes for an alien in the land
But soon shall prove a Theban, native born.
And yet his fortune brings him little joy;
For blind of seeing, clad in beggar's weeds,

For purple robes, and leaning on his staff,
To a strange land he soon shall grope his way.
And of the children, inmates of his home,
He shall be proved the brother and the sire,
Of her who bare him son and husband both,
Co-partner and assassin of his sire.
Go in and ponder this, and if thou find
That I have missed the mark, henceforth declare
I have no wit nor skill in prophecy.

> [*Exeunt* TEIRESIAS *and* OEDIPUS

CHORUS

Who is he by voice immortal named from Pythia's rocky
  cell,
Doer of foul deeds of bloodshed, horrors that no tongue can
  tell?
        A foot for flight he needs
        Fleeter than storm-swift steeds,
        For on his heels doth follow,
Armed with the lightnings of his Sire, Apollo.
        Like sleuth-hounds too
        The Fates pursue.

Yea, but now flashed forth the summons from Parnassus'
  snowy peak,
"Near and far the undiscovered doer of this murder seek!"
        Now like a sullen bull he roves
        Through forest brakes and upland groves,
        And vainly seeks to fly
        The doom that ever nigh
        Flits o'er his head,
Still by the avenging Phoebus sped,
        The voice divine,
        From Earth's mid shrine.

Sore perplexèd am I by the words of the master seer.
Are they true, are they false? I know not and bridle my
   tongue for fear,
Fluttered with vague surmise; nor present nor future is
   clear.
Quarrel of ancient date or in days still near know I none
Twixt the Labdacidan house and our ruler, Polybus' son.
Proof is there none: how then can I challenge our King's
   good name,
How in a blood-feud join for an untracked deed of shame?

All wise are Zeus and Apollo, and nothing is hid from their
   ken;
They are gods; and in wits a man may surpass his fellow
   men;
But that a mortal seer knows more than I know—where
Hath this been proven? Or how without sign assured, can
   I blame
Him who saved our State when the wingèd songstress
   came,
Tested and tried in the light of us all, like gold assayed?
How can I now assent when a crime is on Oedipus laid?

CREON

Friends, countrymen, I learn King Oedipus
Hath laid against me a most grievous charge,
And come to you protesting. If he deems
That I have harmed or injured him in aught
By word or deed in this our present trouble,
I care not to prolong my span of life,
Thus ill-reputed; for the calumny
Hits not a single blot, but blasts my name,

If by the general voice I am denounced
False to the State and false by you my friends.

CHORUS

This taunt, it well may be, was blurted out
In petulance, not spoken advisedly.

CREON

Did any dare pretend that it was I
Prompted the seer to utter a forged charge?

CHORUS

Such things were said; with what intent I know not.

CREON

Were not his wits and vision all astray
When upon me he fixed this monstrous charge?

CHORUS

I know not; to my sovereign's acts I am blind.
But lo, he comes to answer for himself.
Enter OEDIPUS.

OEDIPUS

Sirrah, what mak'st thou here?   Dost thou presume
To approach my doors, thou brazen-facèd rogue,
My murderer and the filcher of my crown?
Come, answer this, didst thou detect in me
Some touch of cowardice or witlessness,
That made thee undertake this enterprise?
I seemed forsooth too simple to perceive
The serpent stealing on me in the dark,
Or else too weak to scotch it when I saw.

'Tis *thou* art witless seeking to possess
Without a following or friends the crown,
A prize that followers and wealth must win.

CREON

Attend me. Thou hast spoken, 'tis my turn
To make reply. Then having heard me, judge.

OEDIPUS

Thou art glib of tongue, but I am slow to learn
Of thee; I know too well thy venomous hate.

CREON

First I would argue out this very point.

OEDIPUS

O argue not that thou art not a rogue.

CREON

If thou dost count a virtue stubbornness,
Unschooled by reason, thou art much astray.

OEDIPUS

If thou dost hold a kinsman may be wronged,
And no pains follow, thou art much to seek.

CREON

Therein thou judgest rightly, but this wrong
That thou allegest—tell me what it is.

OEDIPUS

Didst thou or didst thou not advise that I
Should call the priest?

CREON

Yes, and I stand to it.

OEDIPUS

Tell me how long it is since Laïus . . .

CREON

Since Laïus . . . ? I follow not thy drift.

OEDIPUS

By violent hands was spirited away.

CREON

In the dim past, a many years agone.

OEDIPUS

Did this same prophet then pursue his craft?

CREON

Yes, skilled as now and in no less repute.

OEDIPUS

Did he at that time ever glance at me?

CREON

Not to my knowledge, not when I was by.

OEDIPUS

But was no search and inquisition made?

CREON

Surely full quest was made, but nothing learnt.

OEDIPUS

Why failed the seer to tell his story *then?*

CREON

I know not, and not knowing hold my tongue.

OEDIPUS

This much thou knowest and canst surely tell.

CREON

What mean'st thou?   All I know I will declare.

OEDIPUS

But for thy prompting never had the seer
Ascribed to me the death of Laïus.

CREON

If so he says thou knowest best; but I
Would put thee to the question in my turn.

OEDIPUS

Question and prove me murderer if thou canst.

CREON

Then let me ask thee, didst thou wed my sister?

OEDIPUS

A fact so plain I cannot well deny.

CREON

And as thy consort queen she shares the throne?

OEDIPUS

I grant her freely all her heart desires.

CREON

And with you twain I share the triple rule?

OEDIPUS

Yea, this it is that proves thee a false friend.

CREON

Not so, if thou wouldst reason with thyself,
As I with myself. First, I bid thee think,
Would any mortal choose a troubled reign
Of terrors rather than secure repose,
If the same power were given him? As for me,
I have no natural craving for the name
Of king, preferring to do kingly deeds,
And so thinks every sober-minded man.
Now all my needs are satisfied through thee,
And I have naught to fear; but were I king,
My acts would oft run counter to my will.
How could a title then have charms for me
Above the sweets of boundless influence?
I am not so infatuate as to grasp
The shadow when I hold the substance fast.
Now all men cry me Godspeed! wish me well,
And every suitor seeks to gain my ear,
If he would hope to win a grace from thee.
Why should I leave the better, choose the worse?
That were sheer madness, and I am not mad.
No such ambition ever tempted me,
Nor would I have a share in such intrigue.

And if thou doubt me, first to Delphi go,
There ascertain if my report was true
Of the god's answer; next investigate
If with the seer I plotted or conspired,
And if it prove so, sentence me to death,
Not by thy voice alone, but mine and thine.
But O condemn me not, without appeal,
On bare suspicion. 'Tis not right to adjudge
Bad men at random good, or good men bad.
I would as lief a man should cast away
The thing he counts most precious, his own life,
As spurn a true friend. Thou wilt learn in time
The truth, for time alone reveals the just;
A villain is detected in a day.

CHORUS

To one who walketh warily his words
Commend themselves; swift counsels are not sure.

OEDIPUS

When with swift strides the stealthy plotter stalks
I must be quick too with my counterplot.
To wait his onset passively, for him
Is sure success, for me assured defeat.

CREON

What then's thy will? To banish me the land?

OEDIPUS

I would not have thee banished, no, but dead,
That men may mark the wages envy reaps.

CREON

I see thou wilt not yield, nor credit me.

OEDIPUS

[None but a fool would credit such as thou.]

CREON

Thou art not wise.

OEDIPUS

Wise for myself at least.

CREON

Why not for me too?

OEDIPUS

Why for such a knave?

CREON

Suppose thou lackest sense.

OEDIPUS

Yet kings must rule.

CREON

Not if they rule ill.

OEDIPUS

O my Thebans, hear him!

CREON

Thy Thebans? am not I a Theban too?

CHORUS

Cease, princes; lo there comes, and none too soon,
Jocasta from the palace. Who so fit

As peacemaker to reconcile your feud?
Enter JOCASTA.

JOCASTA

Misguided princes, why have ye upraised
This wordy wrangle? Are ye not ashamed,
While the whole land lies stricken, thus to voice
Your private injuries? Go in, my lord;
Go home, my brother, and forbear to make
A public scandal of a petty grief.

CREON

My royal sister, Oedipus, thy lord,
Hath bid me choose (O dread alternative!)
An outlaw's exile or a felon's death.

OEDIPUS

Yes, lady; I have caught him practising
Against my royal person his vile arts.

CREON

May I ne'er speed but die accursed, if I
In any way am guilty of this charge.

JOCASTA

Believe him, I adjure thee, Oedipus,
First for his solemn oath's sake, then for mine,
And for thine elders' sake who wait on thee.

CHORUS

Hearken, King, reflect, we pray thee, be not stubborn but
relent.

OEDIPUS

Say to what should I consent?

CHORUS

Respect a man whose probity and troth
Are known to all and now confirmed by oath.

OEDIPUS

Dost know what grace thou cravest?

CHORUS

Yea, I know.

OEDIPUS

Declare it then and make thy meaning plain.

CHORUS

Brand not a friend whom babbling tongues assail;
Let not suspicion 'gainst his oath prevail.

OEDIPUS

Bethink you that in seeking this ye seek
In very sooth my death or banishment?

CHORUS

No, by the leader of the host divine!
Witness, thou Sun, such thought was never mine,
Unblest, unfriended may I perish,
If ever I such wish did cherish!
But O my heart is desolate
Musing on our stricken State,
Doubly fall'n should discord grow
Twixt you twain, to crown our woe.

OEDIPUS

Well, let him go, no matter what it cost me,
Or certain death or shameful banishment,
For your sake I relent, not his; and him,
Where'er he be, my heart shall still abhor.

CREON

Thou art as sullen in thy yielding mood
As in thine anger thou wast truculent.
Such tempers justly plague themselves the most.

OEDIPUS

Leave me in peace and get thee gone.

CREON

                              I go,
By thee misjudged, but justified by these.

                                        [*Exit* CREON.

CHORUS

Lady, lead indoors thy consort; wherefore longer here de-
    lay?

JOCASTA

Tell me first how rose the fray.

CHORUS

Rumours bred unjust suspicions and injustice rankles sore.

JOCASTA

Were both at fault then?

CHORUS

                   Both.

JOCASTA

What was the tale?

CHORUS

Ask me no more. The land is sore distressed;
'Twere better sleeping ills to leave at rest.

OEDIPUS

Strange counsel, friend! I know thou mean'st me well,
And yet would'st mitigate and blunt my zeal.

CHORUS

King, I say it once again,
Witless were I proved, insane,
If I lightly put away
Thee my country's prop and stay,
Pilot who, in danger sought,
To a quiet haven brought
Our distracted State; and now
Who can guide us right but thou?

JOCASTA

Let me too, I adjure thee, know, O king,
What cause has stirred this unrelenting wrath.

OEDIPUS

I will, for thou art more to me than these.
Lady, the cause is Creon and his plots.

JOCASTA

But what provoked the quarrel? make this clear.

OEDIPUS

He points me out as Laïus' murderer.

JOCASTA

Of his own knowledge or upon report?

OEDIPUS

He is too cunning to commit himself,
And makes a mouthpiece of a knavish seer.

JOCASTA

Then thou mayst ease thy conscience on that score.
Listen and I'll convince thee that no man
Hath scot or lot in the prophetic art.
Here is the proof in brief. An oracle
Once came to Laïus (I will not say
'Twas from the Delphic god himself, but from
His ministers) declaring he was doomed
To perish by the hand of his own son,
A child that should be born to him by me.
Now Laïus—so at least report affirmed—
Was murdered on a day by highwaymen,
No natives, at a spot where three roads meet.
As for the child, it was but three days old,
When Laïus, its ankles pierced and pinned
Together, gave it to be cast away
By others on the trackless mountain side.
So then Apollo brought it not to pass
The child should be his father's murderer,
Or the dread terror find accomplishment,
And Laïus be slain by his own son.
Such was the prophet's horoscope. O king,

Regard it not. Whate'er the god deems fit
To search, himself unaided will reveal.

OEDIPUS

What memories, what wild tumult of the soul
Came o'er me, lady, as I heard thee speak!

JOCASTA

What mean'st thou? What has shocked and startled thee?

OEDIPUS

Methought I heard thee say that Laïus
Was murdered at the meeting of three roads.

JOCASTA

So ran the story that is current still.

OEDIPUS

Where did this happen? Dost thou know the place?

JOCASTA

Phocis the land is called; the spot is where
Branch roads from Delphi and from Daulis meet.

OEDIPUS

And how long is it since these things befell?

JOCASTA

'Twas but a brief while ere thou wast proclaimed
Our country's ruler that the news was brought.

OEDIPUS

O Zeus, what hast thou willed to do with me!

JOCASTA

What is it, Oedipus, that moves thee so?

OEDIPUS

Ask me not yet; tell me the build and height
Of Laïus? Was he still in manhood's prime?

JOCASTA

Tall was he, and his hair was lightly strewn
With silver; and not unlike thee in form.

OEDIPUS

O woe is me! Methinks unwittingly
I laid but now a dread curse on myself.

JOCASTA

What say'st thou? When I look on thee, my king,
I tremble.

OEDIPUS

'Tis a dread presentiment
That in the end the seer will prove not blind.
One further question to resolve my doubt.

JOCASTA

I quail; but ask, and I will answer all.

OEDIPUS

Had he but few attendants or a train
Of armed retainers with him, like a prince?

JOCASTA

They were but five in all, and one of them
A herald; Laïus in a mule-car rode.

OEDIPUS

Alas! 'tis clear as noonday now. But say,
Lady, who carried this report to Thebes?

JOCASTA

A serf, the sole survivor who returned.

OEDIPUS

Haply he is at hand or in the house?

JOCASTA

No, for as soon as he returned and found
Thee reigning in the stead of Laïus slain,
He clasped my hand and supplicated me
To send him to the alps and pastures, where
He might be farthest from the sight of Thebes.
And so I sent him. 'Twas an honest slave
And well deserved some better recompense.

OEDIPUS

Fetch him at once. I fain would see the man.

JOCASTA

He shall be brought; but wherefore summon him?

OEDIPUS

Lady, I fear my tongue has overrun
Discretion; therefore I would question him.

JOCASTA

Well, he shall come, but may not I too claim
To share this burden of thy heart, my king?

OEDIPUS

And thou shalt not be frustrate of thy wish,
Now my imaginings have gone so far.
Who has a higher claim than thou to hear
My tale of dire adventures? Listen then.
My sire was Polybus of Corinth, and
My mother Meropè, a Dorian;
And I was held the foremost citizen,
Till a strange thing befell me, strange indeed,
Yet scarce deserving all the heat it stirred.
A roisterer at some banquet, flown with wine,
Shouted "Thou art no true son of thy sire."
It irked me, but I stomached for the nonce
The insult; on the morrow I sought out
My mother and my sire and questioned them.
They were indignant at the random slur
Cast on my parentage and did their best
To comfort me, but still the venomed barb
Rankled, for still the scandal spread and grew.
So privily without their leave I went
To Delphi, and Apollo sent me back
Baulked of the knowledge that I came to seek.
But other grievous things he prophesied,
Woes, lamentations, mourning, portents dire;
To wit I should defile my mother's bed
And raise up seed too loathsome to behold,
And slay the father from whose loins I sprang.
Warned by the oracle I turned and fled,—
And Corinth henceforth was to me unknown
Save as I knew its region by the stars;—
Whither, I cared not, so I never might
Behold my doom of infamy fulfilled.

And in my wanderings I reached the place
Where, as thy story runs, the king was slain.
Then, lady,—thou shalt hear the very truth—
As I drew near the triple-branching roads,
A herald met me and a man who sat
In a car drawn by colts—as in thy tale—
The man in front and the old man himself
Threatened to thrust me rudely from the path,
Then jostled by the charioteer in wrath
I struck him, and the old man, seeing this,
Watched till I passed and from his car brought down
Full on my head the double-pointed goad.
   Yet was I quits with him and more; one stroke
Of my good staff sufficed to fling him clean
Out of the chariot seat and laid him prone.
And so I slew them every one. But if
Betwixt this stranger there was aught in common
With Laïus, who more miserable than I,
What mortal could you find more god-abhorred?
Wretch whom no sojourner, no citizen
May harbour or address, whom all are bound
To harry from their homes. And this same curse
Was laid on me, and laid by none but me.
Yea with these hands all gory I pollute
The bed of him I slew. Say, am I vile?
Am I not utterly unclean, a wretch
Doomed to be banished, and in banishment
Forgo the sight of all my dearest ones,
And never tread again my native earth;
Or else to wed my mother and slay my sire,
Polybus, who begat me and upreared?
If one should say, this is the handiwork
Of some inhuman power, who could blame

His judgment? But, ye pure and awful gods,
Forbid, forbid that I should see that day!
May I be blotted out from living men
Ere such a plague spot set on me its brand!

CHORUS

We too, O king, are troubled; but till thou
Hast questioned the survivor, still hope on.

OEDIPUS

My hope is faint, but still enough survives
To bid me bide the coming of this herd.

JOCASTA

Suppose him here, what wouldst thou learn of him?

OEDIPUS

I'll tell thee, lady; if his tale agrees
With thine, I shall have escaped calamity.

JOCASTA

And what of special import did I say?

OEDIPUS

In thy report of what the herdsman said
Laïus was slain by robbers; now if he
Still speaks of robbers, not a robber, I
Slew him not; "one" with "many" cannot square.
But if he says one lonely wayfarer,
The last link wanting to my guilt is forged.

JOCASTA

Well, rest assured, his tale ran thus at first,
Nor can he now retract what then he said;

Not I alone but all our townfolk heard it.
E'en should he vary somewhat in his story,
He cannot make the death of Laïus
In any wise jump with the oracle.
For Loxias said expressly he was doomed
To die by my child's hand, but he, poor babe,
He shed no blood, but perished first himself.
So much for divination. Henceforth I
Will look for signs neither to right nor left.

OEDIPUS

Thou reasonest well. Still I would have thee send
And fetch the bondsman hither. See to it.

JOCASTA

That will I straightway. Come, let us within.
I would do nothing that my lord mislikes.
                    [*Exeunt* OEDIPUS *and* JOCASTA.

CHORUS

My lot be still to lead
    The life of innocence and fly
Irreverence in word or deed,
    To follow still those laws ordained on high
Whose birthplace is the bright ethereal sky
    No mortal birth they own,
    Olympus their progenitor alone:
Ne'er shall they slumber in oblivion cold,
The god in them is strong and grows not old.

    Of insolence is bred
The tyrant; insolence full blown,
    With empty riches surfeited,

Scales the precipitous height and grasps the throne,
    Then topples o'er and lies in ruin prone;
    No foothold on that dizzy steep.
But O may Heaven the true patriot keep
Who burns with emulous zeal to serve the State.
God is my help and hope, on him I wait.

But the proud sinner, or in word or deed,
    That will not Justice heed,
    Nor reverence the shrine
    Of images divine,
Perdition seize his vain imaginings,
    If, urged by greed profane,
    He grasps at ill-got gain,
And lays an impious hand on holiest things.
    Who when such deeds are done
    Can hope heaven's bolts to shun?
If sin like this to honour can aspire,
Why dance I still and lead the sacred choir?

No more I'll seek earth's central oracle,
    Or Abae's hallowed cell,
    Nor to Olympia bring
    My votive offering,
If before all God's truth be not made plain.
    O Zeus, reveal thy might,
    King, if thou'rt named aright
Omnipotent, all-seeing, as of old;
    For Laïus is forgot;
    His weird, men heed it not;
Apollo is forsook and faith grows cold.
Enter JOCASTA.

JOCASTA

My lords, ye look amazed to see your queen
With wreaths and gifts of incense in her hands.
I had a mind to visit the high shrines,
For Oedipus is overwrought, alarmed
With terrors manifold.   He will not use
His past experience, like a man of sense,
To judge the present need, but lends an ear
To any croaker if he augurs ill.
Since then my counsels naught avail, I turn
To thee, our present help in time of trouble,
Apollo, Lord Lycean, and to thee
My prayers and supplications here I bring.
Lighten us, lord, and cleanse us from this curse!
For now we all are cowed like mariners
Who see their helmsman dumbstruck in the storm.
Enter CORINTHIAN MESSENGER.

MESSENGER

My masters, tell me where the palace is
Of Oedipus; or better, where's the king.

CHORUS

Here is the palace and he bides within;
This is his queen the mother of his children.

MESSENGER

All happiness attend her and the house,
Blessed is her husband and her marriage-bed.

JOCASTA

My greetings to thee, stranger; thy fair words

Deserve a like response. But tell me why
Thou comest—what thy need or what thy news.

MESSENGER

Good for thy consort and the royal house.

JOCASTA

What may it be? Whose messenger art thou?

MESSENGER

From Corinth I. The message wherewithal
I stand entrusted thou shalt hear anon.
'Twill please thee surely, yet perchance offend.

JOCASTA

Declare it and explain this double sense.

MESSENGER

The Isthmian commons have resolved to make
Thy husband king—so 'twas reported there.

JOCASTA

What! is not aged Polybus still king?

MESSENGER

No, verily; he's dead and in his grave.

JOCASTA

What! is he dead, the sire of Oedipus?

MESSENGER

If I speak falsely, may I die myself.

JOCASTA

Quick, maiden, bear these tidings to my lord.
Ye god-sent oracles, where stand ye now!
This is the man whom Oedipus long shunned,
In dread to prove his murderer; and now
He dies in nature's course, not by his hand.
Enter OEDIPUS.

OEDIPUS

My wife, my queen, Jocasta, why hast thou
Summoned me from my palace?

JOCASTA

Hear this man,
And as thou hearest judge what has become
Of all those awe-inspiring oracles.

OEDIPUS

Who is this man, and what his news for me?

JOCASTA

He comes from Corinth and his message this:
Thy father Polybus hath passed away.

OEDIPUS

What? let me have it, stranger, from thy mouth.

MESSENGER

If I must first make plain beyond a doubt
My message, know that Polybus is dead.

OEDIPUS

By treachery, or by sickness visited?

MESSENGER

One touch will send an old man to his rest.

OEDIPUS

So of some malady he died, poor man.

MESSENGER

Yes, having measured the full span of years.

OEDIPUS

Out on it, lady! why should one regard
The Pythian hearth or birds that scream i' the air?
Did they not point at me as doomed to slay
My father? but he's dead and in his grave
And here am I who ne'er unsheathed a sword;
Unless the longing for his absent son
Killed him and so *I* slew him in a sense.
But, as they stand, the oracles are dead—
Dust, ashes, nothing, dead as Polybus.

JOCASTA

Say, did not I foretell this long ago?

OEDIPUS

Thou didst: but I was misled by my fear.

JOCASTA

Then let it no more weigh upon thy soul.

OEDIPUS

Must I not fear my mother's marriage bed?

JOCASTA

Why should a mortal man, the sport of chance,
With no assured foreknowledge, be afraid?
Best live a careless life from hand to mouth.
This wedlock with thy mother fear not thou.
How oft it chances that in dreams a man
Has wed his mother! He who least regards
Such brainsick phantasies lives most at ease.

OEDIPUS

I should have shared in full thy confidence,
Were not my mother living; since she lives
Though half convinced I still must live in dread.

JOCASTA

And yet thy sire's death lights our darkness much.

OEDIPUS

Much, but my fear is touching her who lives.

MESSENGER

Who may this woman be whom thus you fear?

OEDIPUS

Meropè, stranger, wife of Polybus.

MESSENGER

And what of her can cause you any fear?

OEDIPUS

A heaven-sent oracle of dread import.

MESSENGER

A mystery, or may a stranger hear it?

OEDIPUS

Aye, 'tis no secret. Loxias once foretold
That I should mate with mine own mother, and shed
With my own hands the blood of my own sire.
Hence Corinth was for many a year to me
A home far distant; and I throve abroad,
But missed the sweetest sight, my parents' face.

MESSENGER

Was this the fear that exiled thee from home?

OEDIPUS

Yea, and the dread of slaying my own sire.

MESSENGER

Why, since I came to give thee pleasure, King,
Have I not rid thee of this second fear?

OEDIPUS

Well, thou shalt have due guerdon for thy pains.

MESSENGER

Well, I confess what chiefly made me come
Was hope to profit by thy coming home.

OEDIPUS

Nay, I will ne'er go near my parents more.

MESSENGER

My son, 'tis plain, thou know'st not what thou doest.

OEDIPUS

How so, old man? For heaven's sake tell me all.

MESSENGER

If this is why thou dreadest to return.

OEDIPUS

Yea, lest the god's word be fulfilled in me.

MESSENGER

Lest through thy parents thou shouldst be accursed?

OEDIPUS

This and none other is my constant dread.

MESSENGER

Dost thou not know thy fears are baseless all?

OEDIPUS

How baseless, if I am their very son?

MESSENGER

Since Polybus was naught to thee in blood.

OEDIPUS

What say'st thou? was not Polybus my sire?

MESSENGER

As much thy sire as I am, and no more.

OEDIPUS

My sire no more to me than one who is naught!

MESSENGER

Since I begat thee not, no more did he.

OEDIPUS

What reason had he then to call me son?

MESSENGER

Know that he took thee from my hands, a gift.

OEDIPUS

Yet, if no child of his, he loved me well.

MESSENGER

A childless man till then, he warmed to thee.

OEDIPUS

A foundling or a purchased slave, this child?

MESSENGER

I found thee in Cithaeron's wooded glens.

OEDIPUS

What led thee to explore those upland glades?

MESSENGER

My business was to tend the mountain flocks.

OEDIPUS

A vagrant shepherd journeying for hire?

MESSENGER

True, but thy saviour in that hour, my son.

OEDIPUS

My saviour? from what harm? what ailed me then?

MESSENGER

Those ankle joints are evidence enow.

OEDIPUS

Ah, why remind me of that ancient sore?

MESSENGER

I loosed the pin that riveted thy feet.

OEDIPUS

Yes, from my cradle that dread brand I bore.

MESSENGER

Whence thou deriv'st the name that still is thine.

OEDIPUS

Who did it? I adjure thee, tell me who.
Say, was it father, mother?

MESSENGER

                    I know not.
The man from whom I had thee may know more.

OEDIPUS

What, did another find me, not thyself?

MESSENGER

Not I; another shepherd gave thee me.

OEDIPUS

Who was he? Would'st thou know again the man?

MESSENGER

He passed indeed for one of Laïus' house.

OEDIPUS

The king who ruled the country long ago?

MESSENGER

The same: he was a herdsman of the king.

OEDIPUS

And is he living still for me to see him?

MESSENGER

His fellow-countrymen should best know that.

OEDIPUS

Doth any bystander among you know
The herd he speaks of, or by seeing him
Afield or in the city? answer straight!
The hour hath come to clear this business up.

CHORUS

Methinks he means none other than the hind
Whom thou anon wert fain to see; but that
Our queen Jocasta best of all could tell.

OEDIPUS

Madam, dost know the man we sent to fetch?
Is he the same of whom the stranger speaks?

JOCASTA

Who is the man? What matter? Let it be.
'Twere waste of thought to weigh such idle words.

OEDIPUS

No, with such guiding clues I cannot fail
To bring to light the secret of my birth.

JOCASTA

Oh, as thou carest for thy life, give o'er
This quest. Enough the anguish *I* endure.

OEDIPUS

Be of good cheer; though I be proved the son
Of a bondwoman, aye, through three descents
Triply a slave, thy honour is unsmirched.

JOCASTA

Yet humour me, I pray thee; do not this.

OEDIPUS

I cannot; I must probe this matter home.

JOCASTA

'Tis for thy sake I advise thee for the best.

OEDIPUS

I grow impatient of this best advice.

JOCASTA

Ah mayst thou ne'er discover who thou art!

OEDIPUS

Go, fetch me here the herd, and leave yon woman
To glory in her pride of ancestry.

JOCASTA

O woe is thee, poor wretch! With that last word
I leave thee, henceforth silent evermore.

[*Exit* JOCASTA

CHORUS

Why, Oedipus, why stung with passionate grief
Hath the queen thus departed? Much I fear
From this dead calm will burst a storm of woes.

OEDIPUS

Let the storm burst, my fixed resolve still holds,
To learn my lineage, be it ne'er so low.
It may be she with all a woman's pride
Thinks scorn of my base parentage. But I
Who rank myself as Fortune's favourite child,
The giver of good gifts, shall not be shamed.
She is my mother and the changing moons
My brethren, and with them I wax and wane.
Thus sprung why should I fear to trace my birth?
Nothing can make me other than I am.

CHORUS

If my soul prophetic err not, if my wisdom aught avail,
     Thee, Cithaeron, I shall hail,
As the nurse and foster-mother of our Oedipus shall greet
Ere to-morrow's full moon rises, and exalt thee as is meet.
Dance and song shall hymn thy praises, lover of our royal
    race.
     Phoebus, may my words find grace!
Child, who bare thee, nymph or goddess? sure thy sire was
    more than man,
     Haply the hill-roamer Pan.
Or did Loxias beget thee, for he haunts the upland wold;
Or Cyllenè's lord, or Bacchus, dweller on the hill-tops cold?
Did some Heliconian Oread give him thee, a new-born joy,
     Nymphs with whom he loves to toy?

OEDIPUS

Elders, if I, who never yet before
Have met the man, may make a guess, methinks
I see the herdsman whom we long have sought;
His time-worn aspect matches with the years
Of yonder agèd messenger; besides
I seem to recognise the men who bring him
As servants of my own. But you, perchance,
Having in past days known or seen the herd,
May better by sure knowledge my surmise.

CHORUS

I recognise him; one of Laïus' house;
A simple hind, but true as any man.
Enter HERDSMAN.

OEDIPUS

Corinthian, stranger, I address thee first,
Is this the man thou meanest!

MESSENGER

This is he.

OEDIPUS

And now, old man, look up and answer all
I ask thee. Wast thou once of Laïus' house?

HERDSMAN

I was, a thrall, not purchased but home-bred.

OEDIPUS

What was thy business? how wast thou employed?

HERDSMAN

The best part of my life I tended sheep.

OEDIPUS

What were the pastures thou didst most frequent?

HERDSMAN

Cithaeron and the neighbouring alps.

OEDIPUS

Then there
Thou must have known yon man, at least by fame?

HERDSMAN

Yon man? in what way? what man dost thou mean?

OEDIPUS

The man here, having met him in past times. . . .

HERDSMAN

Off-hand I cannot call him well to mind.

MESSENGER

No wonder, master. But I will revive
His blunted memories. Sure he can recall
What time together both we drove our flocks,
He two, I one, on the Cithaeron range,
For three long summers; I his mate from spring
Till rose Arcturus; then in winter time
I led mine home, he his to Laïus' folds.
Did these things happen as I say, or no?

HERDSMAN

'Tis long ago, but all thou say'st is true.

MESSENGER

Well, thou must then remember giving me
A child to rear as my own foster-son?

HERDSMAN

Why dost thou ask this question? What of that?

MESSENGER

Friend, he that stands before thee was that child.

HERDSMAN

A plague upon thee! Hold thy wanton tongue!

OEDIPUS

Softly, old man, rebuke him not; thy words
Are more deserving chastisement than his.

HERDSMAN

O best of masters, what is my offence?

OEDIPUS

Not answering what he asks about the child.

HERDSMAN

He speaks at random, babbles like a fool.

OEDIPUS

If thou lack'st grace to speak, I'll loose thy tongue.

HERDSMAN

For mercy's sake abuse not an old man.

OEDIPUS

Arrest the villain, seize and pinion him!

HERDSMAN

Alack, alack!
What have I done? what wouldst thou further learn?

OEDIPUS

Didst give this man the child of whom he asks?

HERDSMAN

I did; and would that I had died that day!

OEDIPUS

And die thou shalt unless thou tell the truth.

HERDSMAN

But, if I tell it, I am doubly lost.

OEDIPUS

The knave methinks will still prevaricate.

HERDSMAN

Nay, I confessed I gave it long ago.

OEDIPUS

Whence came it? was it thine, or given to thee?

HERDSMAN

I had it from another, 'twas not mine.

OEDIPUS

From whom of these our townsmen, and what house?

HERDSMAN

Forbear for God's sake, master, ask no more.

OEDIPUS

If I must question thee again, thou'rt lost.

HERDSMAN

Well then—it was a child of Laïus' house.

OEDIPUS

Slave-born or one of Laïus' own race?

HERDSMAN

Ah me!
I stand upon the perilous edge of speech.

OEDIPUS

And I of hearing, but I still must hear.

HERDSMAN

Know then the child was by repute his own,
But she within, thy consort best could tell.

OEDIPUS

What! she, she gave it thee?

HERDSMAN

                         'Tis so, my king.

OEDIPUS

With what intent?

HERDSMAN

To make away with it.

OEDIPUS

What, she its mother?

HERDSMAN

Fearing a dread weird.

OEDIPUS

What weird?

HERDSMAN

'Twas told that he should slay his sire.

OEDIPUS

Why didst thou give it then to this old man?

HERDSMAN

Through pity, master, for the babe. I thought
He'd take it to the country whence he came;
But he preserved it for the worst of woes.
For if thou art in sooth what this man saith,
God pity thee! thou wast to misery born.

OEDIPUS

Ah me! ah me! all brought to pass, all true!
O light, may I behold thee nevermore!
I stand a wretch, in birth, in wedlock cursed,
A parricide, incestuous, triply cursed.

[*Exit* OEDIPUS

Races of mortal man
Whose life is but a span,
I count ye but the shadow of a shade!
For he who most doth know
Of bliss, hath but the show;
A moment, and the visions pale and fade.
Thy fall, O Oedipus, thy piteous fall
Warns me none born of woman blest to call.

For he of marksmen best,
O Zeus, outshot the rest,
And won the prize supreme of wealth and power.
By him the vulture maid
Was quelled, her witchery laid;
He rose our saviour and the land's strong tower.
We hailed thee king and from that day adored
Of mighty Thebes the universal lord.

O heavy hand of fate!
Who now more desolate,
Whose tale more sad than thine, whose lot more dire?
O Oedipus, discrownèd head,
Thy cradle was thy marriage bed;
One harbourage sufficed for son and sire.
How could the soil thy father eared so long
Endure to bear in silence such a wrong?

All-seeing Time hath caught
Guilt, and to justice brought
The son and sire commingled in one bed.
O child of Laïus' ill-starred race
Would I had ne'er beheld thy face!

I raise for thee a dirge as o'er the dead.
Yet, sooth to say, through thee I drew new breath,
And now through thee I feel a second death.
Enter SECOND MESSENGER.

SECOND MESSENGER

Most grave and reverend senators of Thebes,
What deeds ye soon must hear, what sights behold!
How will ye mourn, if, true-born patriots,
Ye reverence still the race of Labdacus!
Not Ister nor all Phasis' flood, I ween,
Could wash away the blood-stains from this house,
The ills it shrouds or soon will bring to light,
Ills wrought of malice, not unwittingly.
The worst to bear are self-inflicted wounds.

CHORUS

Grievous enough for all our tears and groans
Our past calamities; what canst thou add?

SECOND MESSENGER

My tale is quickly told and quickly heard.
Our sovereign lady queen Jocasta's dead.

CHORUS

Alas, poor queen! how came she by her death?

SECOND MESSENGER

By her own hand. And all the horror of it,
Not having seen, ye cannot apprehend.
Nathless, as far as my poor memory serves,
I will relate the unhappy lady's woe.
When in her frenzy she had passed inside
The vestibule, she hurried straight to win

The bridal-chamber, clutching at her hair
With both her hands, and, once within the room,
She shut the doors behind her with a crash.
"Laïus," she cried, and called her husband dead
Long, long ago; her thought was of that child
By him begot, the son by whom the sire
Was murdered and the mother left to breed
With her own seed, a monstrous progeny.
Then she bewailed the marriage bed whereon
Poor wretch, she had conceived a double brood,
Husband by husband, children by her child.
What happened after that I cannot tell,
Nor how the end befel, for with a shriek
Burst on us Oedipus; all eyes were fixed
On Oedipus, as up and down he strode,
Nor could we mark her agony to the end.
For stalking to and fro "A sword!" he cried,
"Where is the wife, no wife, the teeming womb
That bore a double harvest, me and mine?"
And in his frenzy some supernal power
(No mortal, surely, none of us who watched him)
Guided his footsteps; with a terrible shriek,
As though one beckoned him, he crashed against
The folding doors, and from their staples forced
The wrenchèd bolts and hurled himself within.
Then we beheld the woman hanging there,
A running noose entwined about her neck.
But when he saw her, with a maddened roar
He loosed the cord; and when her wretched corpse
Lay stretched on earth, what followed—O 'twas dread!
He tore the golden brooches that upheld
Her queenly robes, upraising them high and smote
Full on his eye-balls, uttering words like these:

"No more shall ye behold such sights of woe,
Deeds I have suffered and myself have wrought;
Henceforward quenched in darkness shall ye see
Those ye should ne'er have seen; now blind to those
Whom, when I saw, I vainly yearned to know."
Such was the burden of his moan, whereto,
Not once but oft, he struck with hand uplift
His eyes, and at each stroke the ensanguined orbs
Bedewed his beard, not oozing drop by drop,
But one black gory downpour, thick as hail.
Such evils, issuing from the double source,
Have whelmed them both, confounding man and wife.
Till now the storied fortune of this house
Was fortunate indeed; but from this day
Woe, lamentation, ruin, death, disgrace,
All ills that can be named, all, all are theirs.

CHORUS

But hath he still no respite from his pain?

SECOND MESSENGER

He cries, "Unbar the doors and let all Thebes
Behold the slayer of his sire, his mother's—"
That shameful word my lips may not repeat.
He vows to fly self-banished from the land,
Nor stay to bring upon his house the curse
Himself had uttered; but he has no strength
Nor one to guide him, and his torture's more
Than man can suffer, as yourselves will see.
For lo, the palace portals are unbarred,
And soon ye shall behold a sight so sad
That he who most abhorred would pity it.
Enter OEDIPUS *blinded.*

CHORUS

Woeful sight! more woeful none
These sad eyes have looked upon.
Whence this madness?   None can tell
Who did cast on thee his spell,
Prowling all thy life around,
Leaping with a demon bound.
Hapless wretch! how can I brook
On thy misery to look?
Though to gaze on thee I yearn,
Much to question, much to learn,
Horror-struck away I turn.

OEDIPUS

Ah me! ah woe is me!
Ah whither am I borne!
How like a ghost forlorn
My voice flits from me on the air!
On, on the demon goads.   The end, ah where?

CHORUS

An end too dread to tell, too dark to see.

OEDIPUS

Dark, dark!   The horror of darkness, like a shroud,
Wraps me and bears me on through mist and cloud.
Ah me, ah me!   What spasms athwart me shoot,
What pangs of agonising memory!

CHORUS

No marvel if in such a plight thou feel'st
The double weight of past and present woes.

OEDIPUS

Ah friend, still loyal, constant still and kind,
        Thou carest for the blind.
I know thee near, and though bereft of eyes,
        Thy voice I recognize.

CHORUS

O doer of dread deeds, how couldst thou mar
Thy vision thus?   What demon goaded thee?

OEDIPUS

Apollo, friends, Apollo, he it was
        That brought these ills to pass;
But the right hand that dealt the blow
        Was mine, none other.   How,
How could I longer see when sight
        Brought no delight?

CHORUS

Alas! 'tis as thou sayest.

OEDIPUS

Say, friends, can any look or voice
Or touch of love henceforth my heart rejoice?
        Haste, friends, no fond delay,
        Take the twice cursed away
            Far from all ken,
The man abhorred of gods, accursed of men.

CHORUS

O thy despair well suits thy desperate case.
Would I had never looked upon thy face!

OEDIPUS

My curse on him whoe'er unrived
The waif's fell fetters and my life revived!
He meant me well, yet had he left me there,
He had saved my friends and me a world of care.

CHORUS

I too had wished it so.

OEDIPUS

Then had I never come to shed
My father's blood nor climbed my mother's bed;
The monstrous offspring of a womb defiled,
Co-mate of him who gendered me, and child.
Was ever man before afflicted thus,
Like Oedipus.

CHORUS

I cannot say that thou hast counselled well,
For thou wert better dead than living blind.

OEDIPUS

What's done was well done. Thou canst never shake
My firm belief. A truce to argument.
For, had I sight, I know not with what eyes
I could have met my father in the shades,
Or my poor mother, since against the twain
I sinned, a sin no gallows could atone.
Aye, but, ye say, the sight of children joys
A parent's eyes. What, born as mine were born?
No, such a sight could never bring me joy;
Nor this fair city with its battlements,

Its temples and the statues of its gods,
Sights from which I, now wretchedst of all,
Once ranked the foremost Theban in all Thebes,
By my own sentence am cut off, condemned
By my own proclamation 'gainst the wretch,
The miscreant by heaven itself declared
Unclean—and of the race of Laïus.
Thus branded as a felon by myself,
How had I dared to look you in the face?
Nay, had I known a way to choke the springs
Of hearing, I had never shrunk to make
A dungeon of this miserable frame,
Cut off from sight and hearing; for 'tis bliss
To bide in regions sorrow cannot reach.
Why didst thou harbour me, Cithaeron, why
Didst thou not take and slay me? Then I never
Had shown to men the secret of my birth.
O Polybus, O Corinth, O my home,
Home of my ancestors (so wast thou called)
How fair a nursling then I seemed, how foul
The canker that lay festering in the blood!
Now is the blight revealed of root and fruit.
Ye triple high-roads, and thou hidden glen,
Coppice, and pass where meet the three-branched ways,
Ye drank my blood, the life-blood these hands spilt,
My father's; do ye call to mind perchance
Those deeds of mine ye witnessed and the work
I wrought thereafter when I came to Thebes?
O fatal wedlock, thou didst give me birth,
And, having borne me, sowed again my seed,
Mingling the blood of fathers, brothers, children,
Brides, wives and mothers, an incestuous brood,

All horrors that are wrought beneath the sun,
Horrors so foul to name them were unmeet.
O, I adjure you, hide me anywhere
Far from this land, or slay me straight, or cast me
Down to the depths of ocean out of sight.
Come hither, deign to touch an abject wretch;
Draw near and fear not; I myself must bear
The load of guilt that none but I can share.
Enter CREON.

CREON

Lo, here is Creon, the one man to grant
Thy prayer by action or advice, for he
Is left the State's sole guardian in thy stead.

OEDIPUS

Ah me! what words to accost him can I find?
What cause has he to trust me?   In the past
I have been proved his rancorous enemy.

CREON

Not in derision, Oedipus, I come
Nor to upbraid thee with thy past misdeeds.
          (*To* BYSTANDERS)
But shame upon you! if ye feel no sense
Of human decencies, at least revere
The Sun whose light beholds and nurtures all.
Leave not thus nakedly for all to gaze at
A horror neither earth nor rain from heaven
Nor light will suffer. Lead him straight within,
For it is seemly that a kinsman's woes
Be heard by kin and seen by kin alone.

OEDIPUS

O listen, since thy presence comes to me
A shock of glad surprise—so noble thou,
And I so vile—O grant me one small boon.
I ask it not on my behalf, but thine.

CREON

And what the favour thou wouldst crave of me?

OEDIPUS

Forth from thy borders thrust me with all speed;
Set me within some vasty desert where
No mortal voice shall greet me any more.

CREON

This had I done already, but I deemed
It first behoved me to consult the god.

OEDIPUS

His will was set forth fully—to destroy
The parricide, the scoundrel; and I am he.

CREON

Yea, so he spake, but in our present plight
'Twere better to consult the god anew.

OEDIPUS

Dare ye inquire concerning such a wretch?

CREON

Yea, for thyself wouldst credit now his word.

OEDIPUS

Aye, and on thee in all humility
I lay this charge: let her who lies within
Receive such burial as thou shalt ordain;
Such rites 'tis thine, as brother, to perform.
But for myself, O never let my Thebes,
The city of my sires, be doomed to bear
The burden of my presence while I live.
No, let me be a dweller on the hills,
On yonder mount Cithaeron, famed as mine,
My tomb predestined for me by my sire
And mother, while they lived, that I may die
Slain as they sought to slay me, when alive.
This much I know full surely, nor disease
Shall end my days, nor any common chance;
For I had ne'er been snatched from death, unless
I was predestined to some awful doom.
   So be it. I reck not how Fate deals with me.
But my unhappy children—for my sons
Be not concerned, O Creon, they are men,
And for themselves, where'er they be, can fend.
But for my daughters twain, poor innocent maids,
Who ever sat beside me at the board
Sharing my viands, drinking of my cup,
For them, I pray thee, care, and, if thou willst,
O might I feel their touch and make my moan.
Hear me, O prince, my noble-hearted prince!
Could I but blindly touch them with my hands
I'd think they still were mine, as when I saw.
ANTIGONE *and* ISMENE *are led in.*
What say I? can it be my pretty ones
Whose sobs I hear? Has Creon pitied me
And sent me my two darlings? Can this be?

CREON

'Tis true; 'twas I procured thee this delight,
Knowing the joy they were to thee of old.

OEDIPUS

God speed thee! and as meed for bringing them
May Providence deal with thee kindlier
Than it has dealt with me! O children mine,
Where are ye? Let me clasp you with these hands,
A brother's hands, a father's; hands that made
Lack-lustre sockets of his once bright eyes;
Hands of a man who blindly, recklessly,
Became your sire by her from whom he sprang.
Though I cannot behold you, I must weep
In thinking of the evil days to come,
The slights and wrongs that men will put upon you.
Where'er ye go to feast or festival,
No merrymaking will it prove for you,
But oft abashed in tears ye will return.
And when ye come to marriageable years,
Where's the bold wooer who will jeopardize
To take unto himself such disrepute
As to my children's children still must cling,
For what of infamy is lacking here?
"Their father slew his father, sowed the seed
Where he himself was gendered, and begat
These maidens at the source wherefrom he sprang."
Such are the gibes that men will cast at you.
Who then will wed you? None, I ween, but ye
Must pine, poor maids, in single barrenness.
O Prince, Menoeceus' son, to thee I turn,
With thee it rests to father them, for we
Their natural parents, both of us, are lost.

O leave them not to wander poor, unwed,
Thy kin, nor let them share my low estate.
O pity them so young, and but for thee
All destitute. Thy hand upon it, Prince.
To you, my children, I had much to say,
Were ye but ripe to hear. Let this suffice:
Pray ye may find some home and live content,
And may your lot prove happier than your sire's.

CREON

Thou hast had enough of weeping; pass within.

OEDIPUS

I must obey,
Though 'tis grievous.

CREON

Weep not, everything must have its day.

OEDIPUS

Well, I go, but on conditions.

CREON

What thy terms for going, say.

OEDIPUS

Send me from the land an exile.

CREON

Ask this of the gods, not me.

OEDIPUS

But I am the gods' abhorrence.

CREON

Then they soon will grant thy plea.

OEDIPUS

So thou yieldest to my pleading?

CREON

When I speak I mean it so.

OEDIPUS

Lead me hence, then, I am willing.

CREON

Come, but let thy children go.

OEDIPUS

Rob me not of these my children!

CREON

Crave not mastery in all,
For the mastery that raised thee was thy bane and wrought
thy fall.

CHORUS

Look ye, countrymen and Thebans, this is Oedipus the
great,
He who knew the Sphinx's riddle and was mightiest in our
state.
Who for all our townsmen gazed not on his fame with
envious eyes?
Now, in what a sea of troubles sunk and overwhelmed he
lies!

Therefore wait to see life's ending ere thou count one mortal blest;
Wait till free from pain and sorrow he has gained his final rest.

MEDEA

BY

EURIPIDES

DRAMATIS PERSONÆ

Nurse of Medea's Children.
Children's Guardian.[1]

Medea.
Chorus of Corinthian Ladies.
Creon, *King of Corinth*.
Jason.
Aegeus, *King of Athens*.
Messenger.
Children of Medea.

The Scene is in front of Jason's House at Corinth.

---

[1] *Pædagogus.*—A trusted servant, responsible for keeping the boys out of harm's way: he was present at their sports, accompanied them to and from school, and never let them be out of his sight. A similar institution is familiar to Englishmen resident in India.

ARGUMENT

When the Heroes, who sailed in the ship Argo to bring home the Golden Fleece, came to the land of Colchis, they found that to win that treasure was a deed passing the might of mortal man, so terribly was it guarded by monsters magical, even fire-breathing bulls and an unsleeping dragon. But Aphrodite caused Medea the sorceress, daughter of Aeetes the king of the land, to love Jason their captain, so that by her magic he overcame the bulls and the dragon. Then Jason took the Fleece, and Medea withal, for that he had pledged him to wed her in the land of Greece. But as they fled, Absyrtus her brother pursued them with a host of war, yet by Medea's devising was he slain. So they came to the land of Iolcos, and to Pelias, who held the kingdom which was Jason's of right. But Medea by her magic wrought upon Pelias' daughters so that they slew their father. Yet by reason of men's horror of the deed might not Jason and Medea abide in the land, and they came to Corinth. But there all men rejoiced for the coming of a hero so mighty in war and a lady renowned for wisdom unearthly, for that Medea was grandchild of the Sun-god. But after ten years, Creon the king of the land spake to Jason, saying, "Lo, I will give thee my daughter to wife, and thou shalt reign after me, if thou wilt put away thy wife Medea; but her and her two sons will I banish from the land." So Jason consented. And of this befell things strange and awful, which are told herein.

MEDEA

Enter NURSE *of Medea's Children.*

NURSE

WOULD God that Argo's hull had never flown
Through those blue Clashing Rocks to Colchisland,
Nor that the axe-hewn pine in Pelion's glens
Ever had fallen, nor filled with oars the hands
Of hero-princes, who at Pelias' hest
Quested the Golden Fleece! My mistress then,
Medea, ne'er had sailed to Iolcos' towers
With love for Jason thrilled through all her soul,
Nor had on Pelias' daughters wrought to slay
Their sire, nor now in this Corinthian land
Dwelt with her lord and children, gladdening
By this her exile them whose land received her,
Yea, and in all things serving Jason's weal,
Which is the chief salvation of the home,
When wife stands not at variance with her lord.

Now all is hatred: love is sickness-stricken.
For Jason, traitor to his babes and her,
My mistress, weddeth with a child of kings,
Daughter of Creon ruler of the land.
And, slighted thus, Medea, hapless wife,
Cries on the oaths, invokes that mightiest pledge
Of the right hand, and calls the Gods to witness
What recompense from Jason she receives.

147

Fasting, with limbs in grief's abandonment
Flung down, she weeps and wastes through all the days
Since first she knew her lord's wrong done to her,
Never uplifting eye, nor turning ever
From earth her face. No more than rock or sea-wave
Hearkeneth she to friends that counsel her;
Saving at whiles, when, lifting her white neck,
To herself she wails her father once beloved,
Her land, her home, forsaking which she came
Hither with him who holds her now contemned.
Alas for her! she knows, by affliction taught,
How good is fatherland unforfeited.
She loathes her babes, joys not beholding them.
And what she may devise I dread to think.
Grim is her spirit, one that will not brook
Mishandling: yea, I know her, and I fear
Lest to her bridal bower she softly steal,
And through her own heart thrust the whetted knife,
Or slay the king and him that weds his child,
And get herself some doom yet worse thereby;
For dangerous is she: who begins a feud
With her, not soon shall sing the triumph-song.
But lo, her boys, their racing-sport put by,
Draw near, all careless of their mother's wrongs,
For the young heart loves not to brood in grief.
Enter CHILDREN'S GUARDIAN, *with boys.*

CHILDREN'S GUARDIAN

O ancient chattel of my mistress' home,
Why at the gates thus lonely standest thou,
Thyself unto thyself discoursing ills?
How wills Medea to be left of thee?

NURSE

O grey attendant thou of Jason's sons,
The hearts of faithful servants still are touched
By ill-betiding fortunes of their lords.
For I have sunk to such a depth of grief,
That yearning took me hitherward to come
And tell to earth and heaven my lady's plight.

CHILDREN'S GUARDIAN

Ceaseth not yet the hapless one from moan?

NURSE

Cease!—her pain scarce begun, far from its height!

CHILDREN'S GUARDIAN

Ah fool!—if one may say it of his lords—
Little she knoweth of the latest blow.

NURSE

What is it, ancient? Grudge not thou to tell me.

CHILDREN'S GUARDIAN

Naught: I repent me of the word that 'scaped me.

NURSE

Nay, by thy beard, hide not from fellow-thrall—
Silence, if need be, will I keep thereof.

CHILDREN'S GUARDIAN

I heard one saying—feigning not to hear,
As I drew near the old stone seats, where sit
The ancients round Peirene's hallowed fount,—
"Creon, this land's lord, is at point to banish

Mother and sons from soil Corinthian."
Howbeit, if the tale I heard be true
I know not: fain were I it were not so.

NURSE

Will Jason brook such dealing with his sons,
Though from their mother he be wholly estranged?

CHILDREN'S GUARDIAN

Old bonds of love are aye outrun by feet
Of new:—no friend is *he* unto this house.

NURSE

Ruined we are then, if we add fresh ill
To old, ere lightened be our ship of this.

CHILDREN'S GUARDIAN

But thou—for 'tis not season that thy lady
Should know—keep silence, and speak not the tale.

NURSE

Hear, babes, what father this is unto you!
I curse him—not: he is my master still:
But to his friends he stands convict of baseness.

CHILDREN'S GUARDIAN

What man is not?   Hast learnt this only now,
That no man loves his neighbour as himself?
Good cause have some, with most 'tis greed of gain—
As here: their sire for a bride's sake loves not these.

NURSE

Pass in, dear children, for it shall be well.

But thou, keep these apart to the uttermost:
Bring them not nigh their mother angry-souled.
For late I saw her glare, as glares a bull,
On these, as 'twere for mischief; nor her wrath,
I know, shall cease, until its lightning strike.
To foes may she work ill, and not to friends!

MEDEA (*behind the scenes*)

O hapless I! O miseries heaped on mine head!
  Ah me! ah me! would God I were dead!

NURSE

Lo, darlings, the thing that I told you!
  Lo the heart of your mother astir!
And astir is her anger: withhold you
  From her sight, come not nigh unto her.
Haste, get you within: O beware ye
  Of the thoughts as a wild-beast brood,
Of the nature too ruthless to spare ye
      In its desperate mood.

Pass ye within now, departing
  With all speed. It is plain to discern
How a cloud of lamenting, upstarting
  From its viewless beginnings, shall burn
In lightnings of fury yet fiercer.
  What deeds shall be dared of that soul,
So haughty, when wrong's goads pierce her,
      So hard to control?

[*Exeunt* CHILDREN *with* GUARDIAN.

MEDEA (*behind the scenes*)

Woe! I have suffered, have suffered foul wrongs that may
  waken, may waken

Mighty lamentings full well!   O ye children accursed
  from the womb,
Hence to destruction, ye brood of a loathed one forsaken,
  forsaken!
Hence with your father, and perish our home in the black-
  ness of doom!

NURSE

Ah me, in the father's offences
  What part have the babes, that thine hate
Should blast them?—forlorn innocences,
  How sorely I fear for your fate!
How terrible princes' moods are!—
  Long ruling, unschooled to obey,—
Unforgiving, unsleeping their feuds are:
  Better life's level way.

Be it mine, if in greatness I may not,
  In quiet and peace to grow old.
Sweeter name than "The Mean" shall ye say not,
  And to taste it is sweetness untold.
But to men never weal above measure
  Availed: on its perilous height
The Gods in their hour of displeasure
  The heavier smite.
Enter CHORUS *of Corinthian Ladies.*

CHORUS

I have hearkened the voice of the daughter of Colchis, the
  sound of the crying
Of the misery-stricken; nor yet is she stilled.   Now the tale
  of her tell,
Grey woman; for moaned through the porch from her
  chamber the wail of her sighing;

And I cannot, I cannot be glad while the home in affliction
  is lying,
        The house I have loved so well.

NURSE

Home?—home there is none: it hath vanished away:
  For my lord to a bride of the princess is thrall;
And my lady is pining the livelong day
In her bower, and for naught that her friends' lips say
  On her heart may the dews of comfort fall.

MEDEA (behind the scenes)

Would God that the flame of the lightning from heaven
  descending, descending,
  Might burn through mine head!—for in living wherein
    any more is my gain?
Alas and alas! Would God I might bring to an ending, an
  ending,
  The life that I loathe, and behind me might cast all its
    burden of pain!

CHORUS

  O Zeus, Earth, Light, did ye hear her,
    How waileth the woe-laden breath
      Of the bride in unhappiest plight?
      What yearning for vanished delight,
      O passion-distraught, should have might
  To cause thee to wish death nearer—
    The ending of all things, death?
    Make thou not for this supplication!
      If thine husband hath turned and adored
      New love, that estrangèd he is,
      O harrow thy soul not for this:
      It is Zeus that shall right thee, I wis.

Ah, pine not in over-vexation
Of spirit, bewailing thy lord!

MEDEA (*behind the scenes*)

O Lady of Justice, O Artemis' Majesty, see it, O see it—
Look on the wrongs that I suffer, by oaths everlasting
who tied
The soul of mine husband, that ne'er from the curse he
might free it, nor free it
From your vengeance! O may I behold him at last, even
him and his bride,
Them, and these halls therewithal, all shattered in ruin, in
ruin!—
Wretches, who dare unprovoked to do to Medea despite!
O father, O city, whom erst I forsook, for undoing, un-
doing,
And for shame, when the blood of my brother I spilt
on the path of my flight!

NURSE

Do ye hear what she saith, and uplifteth her cry
Unto Themis and Zeus, to the Suppliant's King,
Oath-steward of men that be born but to die?
O my lady will lay not her anger by
Soon, making her vengeance a little thing.

CHORUS

If she would but come forth where we wait her,
If she would but give ear to the sound
Of our speech, that her spirit would learn
From its fierceness of anger to turn,
And her lust for revenge not burn!
O ne'er may my love prove traitor,
Never false to my friends be it found!

Medea

But go thou, and forth of the dwelling
  Thy mistress hitherward lead:
    Say to her that friends be we all.
    O hasten, ere mischief befall
    The lords of the palace-hall;
  For her grief, like a tempest upswelling,
    Resistless shall ruin-ward speed.

NURSE

I will do it: but almost my spirit despaireth
  To win her: yet labour of love shall it be.
But my queen on her thralls as a mad bull glareth,
Or a lioness couched mid her whelps, whoso dareth
  With speech to draw near her, so tameless is she.

He should err not, who named the old singers in singing
  Not cunning, but left-handed bards, for their lays
Did they frame for the mirth-tide, the festal inbringing
Of the wine, and the feast, when the harp-strings are
    ringing
  To sweeten with melody life's sweet days.

But the dread doom of mortals, the anguish heartrending—
  Never minstrel by music hath breathed on them peace,
Nor by song with his harp-notes in harmony blending;
Albeit thereof cometh death's dark ending
  Unto many a home that is wrecked by these.

And yet were it surely a boon to bring healing
  Of sorrow to mortals with song; but in vain
Mid the fulness of feasting ring voices clear-pealing,
And the banquet itself hath a glamour, concealing
  From mortals their doom, flinging spells over pain.
                                            [*Exit* NURSE.

CHORUS

I have heard it, the sigh-laden cry of the daughter
  Of Colchis, the woe-shrilling anguish of wailing
For the traitor to love who with false vows caught her
    Who in strength of her wrongs chideth Heaven, assailing
    The Oath-queen of Zeus, who with cords all-prevailing
Forth haled her, and brought her o'er star-litten water,
        Where the brine-mists hover o'er Pontus' Key,
        Unto Hellas far over the boundless sea.
Enter MEDEA.

MEDEA

Corinthian dames, I have come forth my doors
Lest ye condemn me. Many I know are held
Mis-proud—some, since they shrink from public gaze;
Some, from their bearing to their fellow-men;
Some quiet lives for indolence are defamed;
For justice dwells not in the eyes of man,
Who, ere he hath discerned his neighbour's heart,
Hates him at sight, albeit nowise wronged.
A stranger must conform to the city's wont;
Nor citizens uncondemned may flout their fellows.
Like mannerless churls, a law unto themselves.

But me—the blow ye wot of suddenly fell
Soul-shattering. 'Tis my ruin: I have lost
All grace of life: I long to die, O friends.
He, to know whom well was mine all in all,
My lord, of all men basest hath become!
Surely, of creatures that have life and wit,
We women are of all unhappiest,
Who, first must buy, as buys the highest bidder,
A husband—nay, we do but win for our lives

A master!   Deeper depth of wrong is this.
Here too is dire risk—will the lord we gain
Be evil or good?   Divorce?—'tis infamy
To us: we may not even reject a suitor! [1]

Then, coming to new customs, habits new,
One need be a seer, to know the thing unlearnt
At home, what manner of man her mate shall be.
And *if* we learn our lesson, *if* our lord
Dwell with us, plunging not against the yoke,
Happy our lot is; else—no help but death.
For the man, when the home-yoke galls his neck,
Goes forth, to ease a weary sickened heart
By turning to some friend, some kindred soul:
We to one heart alone can look for comfort.

But we, say they, live an unperilled life
At home, while they do battle with the spear—
Unreasoning fools!   Thrice would I under shield
Stand, rather than bear childbirth-peril once.

But ah, thy story is not one with mine!
Thine is this city, thine a father's home,
Thine bliss of life and fellowship of friends;
But I, lone, cityless, and outraged thus
Of him who kidnapped me from foreign shores,
Mother nor brother have I, kinsman none,
For port of refuge from calamity.
Wherefore I fain would win of thee this boon:—
If any path be found me, or device,
Whereby to avenge these wrongs upon mine husband,
On her who weds, on him who gives the bride,

---

[1] A Greek girl's husband was chosen for her by her parents.

Keep silence. Woman quails at every peril,
Faint-heart to face the fray and look on steel;
But when in wedlock-rights she suffers wrong,
No spirit more bloodthirsty shall be found.

CHORUS

This will I; for 'tis just that thou, Medea,
Requite thy lord: no marvel thou dost grieve.
But I see Creon, ruler of this land,
Advancing, herald of some new decree.
Enter CREON.

CREON

Black-lowering woman, wroth against thy lord,
Medea, forth this land I bid thee fare
An exile, taking thy two sons with thee;
And make no tarrying: daysman of this cause
Am I, and homeward go I not again
Ere from the land's bounds I have cast thee forth.

MEDEA

Ah me! undone am I in utter ruin!
My foes crowd sail pursuing: landing-place
Is none from surges of calamity.
Yet, howso wronged, one question will I ask—
For what cause, Creon, dost thou banish me?

CREON

I fear thee—need is none to cloak my words—
Lest thou wreak cureless vengeance on my child.
And to this dread do many things conspire:
Wise art thou, cunning in much evil lore;

Chafed art thou, of thine husband's couch bereft:
I hear thou threatenest, so they bring me word,
To wreak on sire, on bridegroom, and on bride
Mischief. I guard mine head ere falls the blow.
Better be hated, woman, now of thee,
Than once relent, and sorely groan too late.

MEDEA

Not now first, Creon,—many a time ere now
Rumour hath wronged and wrought me grievous harm.
Ne'er should the man whose heart is sound of wit
Let teach his sons more wisdom than the herd.
They are burdened with unprofitable lore,
And spite and envy of other folk they earn.
For, if thou bring strange wisdom unto dullards,
Useless shalt thou be counted, and not wise:
And, if thy fame outshine those heretofore
Held wise, thou shalt be odious in men's eyes.
Myself too in this fortune am partaker.
Of some my wisdom wins me jealousy,
Some count me spiritless; outlandish some;
Unsocial some. Yet no deep lore is mine.
And thou, thou fear'st me, lest I work thee harm.
Not such am I—O Creon, dread not me—
That against princes I should dare transgress.
How hast thou wronged me? Thou hast given thy child
To whomso pleased thee. But—I hate mine husband;
So, doubtless, this in prudence hast thou done.
Nay, but I grudge not thy prosperity.
Wed ye, and prosper. But in this your land
Still let me dwell: for I, how wronged soe'er,
Will hold my peace, o'ermastered by the strong.

CREON

Soft words to hear!—but in thine inmost heart,
I fear, thou plottest mischief all the while;
And all the less I trust thee than before.
The vehement-hearted woman—yea, or man—
Is easier watched-for than the silent-cunning.
Nay, forth with all speed: plead me pleadings **none;**
For this is stablished: no device hast thou
To bide with us, who art a foe to me.

MEDEA (*clasping his feet*)

Nay,—by thy knees, and by the bride, thy child!

CREON

Thou wastest words; thou never shalt prevail.

MEDEA

Wilt drive me forth, respecting naught my prayers?

CREON

Ay: more I love not thee than mine own house.

MEDEA

My country! O, I call thee now to mind!

CREON

Ay, next my children, dear to me is Corinth.

MEDEA

Alas! to mortals what a curse is love!

CREON

Blessing or curse, I trow, as fortune falls.

MEDEA

Zeus, Zeus, forget not him who is cause of this!

CREON

Hence, passionate fool, and rid me of my trouble.

MEDEA

Troubled am I; new troubles need I none.

CREON

Soon shalt thou be by servants' hands thrust out.

MEDEA

Nay—nay—not this, O Creon, I implore!

CREON

So, woman, thou, it seems, wilt make a coil.

MEDEA

I will flee forth:—not this the boon I crave.

CREON

Why restive then?—why rid not Corinth of thee?

MEDEA

Suffer me yet to tarry this one day,
And somewhat for our exile to take thought,
And find my babes a refuge, since their sire
Cares naught to make provision for his sons.
Compassionate these—a father too art thou
Of children—meet it is thou show them grace.
Not for myself I fret, if I be banished:
For them in their calamity I mourn.

CREON

My spirit least of all is tyrannous.
Many a plan have my relentings marred:
And, woman, now I know I err herein,
Yet shalt thou win this boon. But I forewarn thee,
If thee the approaching Sun-god's torch behold
Within this country's confines with thy sons,
Thou diest:—the word is said that shall not lie.
Now, if remain thou must, remain one day—
Too short for thee to do the deeds I dread.   [*Exit.*

CHORUS

O hapless thou!
Woe's me for thy misery, woe for the trouble and anguish
     that meet thee!
Whitherward wilt thou turn thee?—what welcoming hand
     mid the strangers shall greet thee?
What home or what land to receive thee, deliverance from
     evils to give thee,
          Wilt thou find for thee now?
How mid surge of despair to o'erwhelm thee in ruin
     God's hand on thine helm
          Hath steered, O Medea, thy prow!

MEDEA

Wronged—wronged by God and man! Who shall gainsay?
But is it mere despair?—deem not so yet.
Bridegroom and bride grim wrestlings yet await;
Nor troubles light abide these marriage-makers.
Dost think that I had cringed to yon man ever,
Except to gain some gain, or work some wile?
Nor word nor touch of hand had I vouchsafed him!
But to such height of folly hath he come,

That, when he might forestall mine every plot
By banishment, this day of grace he grants me
To stay, wherein three foes will I lay dead,
The father, and the daughter, and mine husband.
And, having for them many paths of death,
Which first to take in hand I know not, friends—
To fire yon palace midst their marriage-feast,
Or to steal softly to their bridal-bower,
And through their two hearts thrust the whetted knife.
Yet one thing bars the way—if I be found
Crossing the threshold of the house and plotting,
Die shall I mid the mocking laughter of foes.

Best the sure path, wherein my nature's cunning
Excels, by poisons to destroy them—yea.
Now, grant them dead: what city will receive me,
What host vouchsafe a land of refuge, home
Secure, and from the avenger shield my life?
There is none. Tarrying then a little space,
If any tower of safety shall appear,
These deaths by guile and silence will I compass;
But if misfortune drive me desperate forth,
Myself will grip the sword,—yea, though I die,—
And slay, and dare the strong hand's reckless deed.

Ah, by the Queen of Night, whom I revere
Above all, and for fellow-worker chose,
Hecate, dweller by mine hearth's dark shrine,
None, none shall vex my soul, and rue it not.
Bitter and woeful bridal will I give them,
Bitter troth-plight and banishing of me.

Up then!—spare naught of all thy sorcery-lore,
Medea, of thy plotting and contriving;

On to the dread deed! Now is need of daring.
Look on thy wrongs: thou must not make derision
For sons of Sisyphus, for Jason's bride,—
Thou, sprung from royal father, from the Sun!
Thou know'st the means. I prove me woman indeed!
Men say we are most helpless for all good,
But of dark deeds most cunning fashioners.

CHORUS

Upward and back to their fountains the sacred rivers are
    stealing;
  Justice is turned to injustice, the order of old to confusion:
The thoughts of the hearts of men are treachery wholly,
    and, reeling
    From its ancient foundations, the faith of the Gods is
      become a delusion.
Everywhere change!—even me men's voices henceforth
    shall honour;
    My life shall be sunlit with glory; for woman the old-
      time story
Is ended, the slanders hoary no more shall as chains be
    upon her.
And the strains of the singers of old generations for shame
    shall falter,
    Which sang evermore of the treason of woman, her
      faithlessness ever.
Alas, that our lips are not touched with the fire of song
    from the altar
    Of Phoebus, the Harper-king, of the inspiration-giver!
Else had I lifted my voice in challenge of song high-ringing
    Unto men: for the roll of the ages shall find for the poet-
      sages

Proud woman-themes for their pages, heroines worthy their
  singing.
But thou from the ancient home didst sail over leagues
  of foam,
On-sped by a frenzied heart, and the sea-gates sawest dis-
  part,
    The Twin Rocks. Now, in the land
      Of the stranger, thy doom is to waken
      To a widowed couch, and forsaken
      Of thy lord, and woe-overtaken,
    To be cast forth shamed and banned.
Disannulled is the spell of the oath: no shame for the
  broken troth
In Hellas the wide doth remain, but heavenward its flight
  hath it ta'en.
    No home of a father hast thou
      For thine haven when trouble-storms lower.
      Usurped is thy bridal bower
      Of another, in pride of her power,
    Ill-starred, overqueening thee now.
Enter JASON

JASON

Not now first, nay, but ofttimes have I marked
What desperate mischief is a froward spirit.
Thou mightest stay in Corinth, in these halls,
Bearing unfractiously thy rulers' pleasure,
Yet for wild whirling words banished thou art.
Me they vex not—cease never, an thou wilt,
Clamouring, "Jason is of men most base!"
But, for thy railing on thy rulers, count it
All gain, that only exile punisheth thee.
For me—I have striven long to appease the wrath

Of kings incensed: fain would I thou shouldst **stay**.
But thou rein'st not thy folly, speaking still
Evil of dignities; art therefore banished.
Yet, for all this, not wearied of my friends,
With so much forethought come I for thee, lady,
That, banished with thy babes, thou lack not **gold**,
Nor aught beside; for exile brings with it
Hardships full many. Though thou hatest **me**,
Never can I bear malice against thee.

MEDEA

Caitiff of caitiffs!—blackest of reproaches
My tongue for thine unmanliness can frame—
Com'st thou to me—dost come, most hateful **proved**
To heaven, to me, to all the race of men?
This is not daring, no, nor courage this,
To wrong thy friends, and blench not from their **eyes**,
But, of all plagues infecting men, the worst,
Even shamelessness. And yet 'tis well thou cam'st,
For I shall ease the burden of mine heart
Reviling thee, and thou be galled to hear.
And with the first things first will I begin.
I saved thee: this knows every son of Greece
That stepped with thee aboard thine Argo's hull,
Thee, sent to quell the flame-outbreathing bulls
With yoke-bands, and to sow the tilth of death.
The dragon, warder of the Fleece of Gold,
That sleepless kept it with his manifold coils,
I slew, and raised deliverance-light for thee.
Myself forsook my father and mine home,
And to Iolcos under Pelion came
With thee, more zealous in thy cause than wise.
Pelias I slew by his own children's hands—

Of all deaths worst,—and dashed their house to ruin.
Thus dealt with, basest of all men, by me,
For a new bride hast thou forsaken me,
Though I had borne thee children! Wert thou childless,
Not past forgiving were this marriage-craving.
But faith of oaths hath vanished. I know not
Whether thou deem'st the olden Gods yet rule,
Or that new laws are now ordained for men;
For thine heart speaks thee unto me forsworn.
Out on this right hand, which thou oft wouldst clasp,—
These knees!—I was polluted by the touch
Of a base man, thus frustrate of mine hopes!
Come, as a friend will I commune with thee—
Yet what fair dealing should I hope from thee?—
Yet will I: questioned, baser shalt thou show.
Now, whither turn I?—to my father's house,
My land?—which I betrayed, to flee with thee!
To Pelias' hapless daughters? Graciously
Their father's slayer would they welcome home!
For thus it is—a foe am I become
To mine own house: no quarrel I had with those
With whom I have now a death-feud for thy sake.
For all this hast thou made me passing-blest
Midst Hellas' daughters! Oh, in thee have I—
O wretched I!—a wondrous spouse and leal,
Since from the land cast forth I pass to exile
Forlorn of friends, alone with children lone.
A proud reproach for our new bridegroom this—
"In poverty his babes, his saviour, wander!"
O Zeus, ah wherefore hast thou given to men
Plain signs for gold which is but counterfeit,
But no assay-mark nature-graven shows
On man's form, to discern the base withal?

CHORUS

Awful and past all healing is that wrath
When they that once loved clash in feud of hate.

JASON

Needs must I be not ill at speech, meseems,
But, like the careful helmsman of a ship,
With close-reefed canvas run before the gale,
Woman, of thy tempestuous-railing tongue.
I—for thy kindness tower-high thou pilest—
Deem Cypris saviour of my voyaging,
Her, and none other or of Gods or men.
Thou art subtle of wit—nay, but ungenerous
It were to tell how Love, by strong compulsion
Of shafts unerring, made thee save my life.
Yet take I not account too strict thereof;
For, in that thou didst save me, thou didst well.
Howbeit, more hast thou received than given
From my deliverance, as my words shall prove:—
First, then, in Hellas dwell'st thou, in the stead
Of land barbaric, knowest justice, learnest
To live by law without respect of force;
And all the Greeks have heard thy wisdom's fame.
Renown is thine; but if on earth's far bourn
Thou dwelledst yet, thou hadst not lived in story.
Now mine be neither gold mine halls within,
Nor sweeter song be mine than Orpheus sang,
If my fair fortune be to fame unknown.

Thus far of my great labours have I spoken,—
This challenge to debate didst thou fling down:—
But, for thy railings on my royal marriage,
Herein will I show, first, that wise I was;

Then, temperate; third, to thee the best of friends
And to my children—nay, but hear me out.

When I came hither from Iolcos-land
With many a desperate fortune in my train,
What happier treasure-trove could I have found
Than to wed—I, an exile—with a princess?
Not—where it galls thee—loathing couch of thine,
And for a new bride smitten with desire,
Nor eager I to multiply mine offspring:—
Suffice these born to me: no fault in them:
But that—this chiefly—we might live in honour,
And be not straitened,—for I know full well
How all friends from the poor man stand aloof,—
And I might nurture as beseems mine house
Our sons, and to these born of thee beget
Brethren, and, knitting in one family all,
Live happy days. Thou, what wouldst thou of **children?**
But me it profits, through sons to be born
To help the living. Have I planned so ill?
Not thou wouldst say it, save for jealousy's sting.

But ye—ye women—so unreasoning are
That, wedlock-rights untrespassed-on, all's **well;**
But, if once your sole tenure be infringed,
With the best, fairest lot are ye at feud
Most bitter. Would that mortals otherwise
Could get them babes, that womankind were **not,**
And so no curse had lighted upon men.

CHORUS

Words, Jason, words, tricked out full cunningly!
Yet to me—though I speak not to thy mind—
Unjust thou seem'st, betraying thus thy wife.

MEDEA

Not as the world thinks think I oftentimes;
Nay, to my thought, a villain's artful tongue
Doubles the hurt his villainy doth to him:
So sure his tongue can gloze the wrong, he grows
Reckless in sin—a mere fool's wisdom this.

Then be not thou, as touching me, fair-seeming
And crafty-tongued: one word shall overthrow thee:
Thou shouldst, wert thou not base, have wed this bride
With my consent, not hid it from thy friends.

JASON

Ay, this my purpose nobly hadst thou helped,
Had I a marriage named, who even now
Canst not refrain thy heart's exceeding wrath!

MEDEA

Not this thine hindrance, but the alien wife
No crown of honour was as eld drew on.

JASON

Now know this well—not for the woman's sake
I wed the royal bride whom I have won,
But, as I said, of my desire to save
Thee, and beget seed royal, to my sons
Brethren, and for mine house a tower of strength.

MEDEA

No prosperous life 'neath sorrow's cloud for me,
Nor weal, with thorns aye rankling in mine heart!

JASON

Know'st how to change thy prayer, and wiser show?
May thy good never seem to thee thy grief;
Nor in fair fortune deem thy lot misfortune.

MEDEA

O yea, insult! Thou hast a refuge, thou;
But desolate I am banished from this land.

JASON

Thyself hast chosen this: blame none beside.

MEDEA

I?—sooth, by wedding and betraying thee!

JASON

By cursing princes with an impious curse.

MEDEA

Ay—and to *thine* house hast thou found me a curse!

JASON

With thee no more I wrangle touching this.
But if, or for the children or thyself,
For help in exile thou wilt take my gold,
Speak: ready am I to give with hand ungrudging,
And send guest-tokens which shall find thee friends.
If this thou wilt not, foolish shalt thou be:
Refrain wrath, and advantaged shalt thou be.

MEDEA

Thy friends!—nothing will I of friends of thine.
No whit will I receive, nor offer thou.
No profit is there in a villain's gifts.

JASON

In any wise I call the Gods to witness
That all help would I give thee and thy sons;
But thy good likes thee not: thy stubborn pride
Spurns friends: the more thy grief shall therefore be.
[*Exit.*

MEDEA

Away!—impatience for the bride new-trapped
Consumes thee loitering from her bower afar!
Wed: for perchance—and God shall speed the word—
Thine shall be bridal thou wouldst fain renounce.

CHORUS

Love bringeth nor honour nor profit to men when it cometh
    restraining
Not its unscanted excess: but if Cypris, in measure raining
    Her joy, cometh down, there is none other Goddess so
    winsome as she.
Not upon me, O Queen, do thou aim from thy bow all-
    golden
    The arrow desire-envenomed that none may avoid—not
    on me!
But let Temperance shield me, the fairest of gifts of the
    Gods ever-living:
Nor ever with passion of jarring contention, nor feuds
    unforgiving,
    In her terrors may Love's Queen visit me, smiting with
    maddened unrest
For a couch mismated my soul; but the peace of the bride-
    bed be holden
    In honour of her, and her keen eyes choose for us bonds
    that be best.

O fatherland, O mine home,
Not mine be the exile's doom!
Into poverty's pathways hard to be trod may my feet not
be guided!
Most piteous anguish were this.
By death—O by death ere then may the conflict of life be
decided,
Ended be life's little day! To be thus from the home-
land divided—
No pang more bitter there is.
We have seen, and it needeth naught
That of others herein we be taught:
For thee not a city, for thee not a friend hath com-
passionated
When affliction most awful is thine.
But he, who regardeth not friends, accursed may he perish,
and hated,
Who opes not his heart with sincerity's key to the hapless-
fated—
Never such shall be friend of mine.
Enter AEGEUS.

AEGEUS

Medea, joy to thee!—for fairer greeting
None knoweth to accost his friends withal.

MEDEA

Joy to thee also, wise Pandion's son,
Aegeus. Whence art thou journeying through this land?

AEGEUS

Leaving the ancient oracle of Phoebus.

MEDEA

Why didst thou fare to earth's prophetic navel?

AEGEUS

To ask how seed of children might be mine.

MEDEA

'Fore Heaven!—aye childless is thy life till now?

AEGEUS

Childless I am, by chance of some God's will.

MEDEA

This, with a wife, or knowing not the couch?

AEGEUS

Nay, not unyoked to wedlock's bed am I.

MEDEA

Now what to thee spake Phoebus touching issue?

AEGEUS

Deep words of wisdom not for man to interpret.

MEDEA

Without sin might I know the God's reply?

AEGEUS

O yea—good sooth, it asks a wise wit most.

MEDEA

What said he? Say, if sin be not to hear.

AEGEUS

"Loose not the wine-skin's forward-jutting foot"—

MEDEA

Till thou shouldst do what thing, or reach what land?

AEGEUS

"Till to the hearth ancestral back thou come."

MEDEA

And thou, what wouldst thou sailing to this shore?

AEGEUS

There is one Pittheus, king of Troezen he,—

MEDEA

A man most pious, Pelops' son, they say.

AEGEUS

To him the God's response I fain would tell.

MEDEA

Yea—a wise man, who hath much skill therein.

AEGEUS

Yea, and my best-belovèd spear-ally.

MEDEA

Now prosper thou, and win thine heart's desire.

AEGEUS

Why droops thine eye?—why this wan-wasted hue?

MEDEA

Aegeus, of all men basest is mine husband.

AEGEUS

What say'st thou?   Clearly tell me thine heart's pain.

MEDEA

He wrongs me—Jason, never wronged of me.

AEGEUS

What hath he done?   More plainly tell it out.

MEDEA

Another wife he takes, his household's queen.

AEGEUS

Ha! hath he dared in truth this basest deed?

MEDEA

Yea: I am now dishonoured, once beloved.

AEGEUS

Another love was this?—or hate of thee?

MEDEA

Love?—deep and high his love is!—traitor in **love!**

AEGEUS

Away with him, if he be base as this!

MEDEA

His love was for affinity with princes.

AEGEUS

Who giveth him his daughter? Tell me all.

MEDEA

Creon, who ruleth this Corinthian land.

AEGEUS

Sooth, lady, reason was that thou shouldst grieve.

MEDEA

'Tis death to me! Yes, also am I banished.

AEGEUS

Of whom? A monstrous wrong thou namest now!

MEDEA

Creon from Corinth driveth me an exile.

AEGEUS

Doth Jason suffer this?—I count it shame!

MEDEA

In pretence, no—yet O, he bears it well!
But I beseech thee, lo, thy beard I touch,—
I clasp thy knees, thy suppliant am I now:—
Pity, O pity me the evil-starred,
And see me not cast forth to homelessness:
Receive to a hearth-place in thy land, thine halls.
So by heaven's blessing fruitful be thy love
In children, and in death thyself be blest.
Thou know'st not what good fortune thou hast found;
For I will end thy childlessness, will cause
Thy seed to grow to sons; such charms I know.

AEGEUS

For many causes am I minded, lady,
This grace to grant thee: for the God's sake first;
Then, for thy promise of a seed of sons;
For herein Aegeus' name is like to die.
But thus it is—if to my land thou come,
I will protect thee all I can: my right
Is this; but I forewarn thee of one thing—
Not from this land to lead thee I consent;
But, if thou reachest of thyself mine halls,
Safe shalt thou bide; to none will I yield thee.
But from this land thou must thyself escape;
For even to strangers blameless will I be.

MEDEA

So be it. Yet, were oath-pledge given for this
To me, then had I all I would of thee.

AEGEUS

Ha, dost not trust me?—or at what dost stumble?

MEDEA

I trust thee; but my foes are Pelias' house
And Creon. Oath-bound, thou couldst never yield me
To these, when they would drag me from the land.
Hadst thou but promised, to the Gods unpledged,
Thou mightest turn their friend, might'st lightly yield
To herald-summons. Strengthless is my cause:
     Wealth is on their side, and a princely house.

AEGEUS

Foresight exceeding, lady, in thy words!
Yet, if this be thy will, I draw not back.

Yea, for myself is this the safest course,
To have a plea to show unto thy foes;
And firmer stands thy cause. The Oath-gods name.

MEDEA

Swear by Earth's plain, and by my father's father,
The Sun, and join the Gods' whole race thereto.

AEGEUS

That I will do or not do—what? Say on.

MEDEA

Never thyself to cast me forth thy land,
Nor, if a foe of mine would hale me thence,
To yield me willingly up, while thou dost live.

AEGEUS

By Earth, the Sun's pure majesty, and all
The Gods, I swear to abide by this thou hast said.

MEDEA

Enough. For broken troth what penalty?

AEGEUS

The worst that scourgeth God-despising men.

MEDEA

Pass on thy way rejoicing: all is well.
I too will come with all speed to thy burg,
When mine intent is wrought, my wish attained.

[*Exit* AEGEUS.

CHORUS

Now the Scion of Maia, the Wayfarer's King,
   Bring thee safe to thine home, and the dream of thine
      heart,
The sweet visions that wing thy feet, mayst thou bring
To accomplishment, Aegeus, for now this thing
   Hath taught me how noble thou art.

MEDEA

O Zeus, Zeus' daughter Justice, Light of the Sun!
Over my foes triumphant now, my friends,
Shall we become: our feet are on the path
Now is there hope of vengeance on my foes.
For this man, there where my chief weakness lay,
Hath for my plots a haven in storm appeared.
To him my bark's stern-hawser make I fast,
To Pallas' burg and fortress when I go.
And all my plots to thee will I tell now;
Nor look I that my words should pleasure thee:—
One of mine household will I send to Jason,
And will entreat him to my sight to come;
And soft words, when he cometh, will I speak,
Saying, "Thy will is mine," and, "It is well";
Saying, his royal marriage, my betrayal,
Is our advantage, and right well devised.
I will petition that my sons may stay—
Not for that I would leave on hostile soil
Children of mine for foes to trample on,
But the king's daughter so by guile to slay.
For I will send them bearing gifts in hand
Unto the bride, that they may not be banished,
A robe fine-spun, a golden diadem.
If she receive and don mine ornaments,

Die shall she wretchedly, and all who touch her;
With drugs so dread will I anoint my gifts.
Howbeit here I pass this story by,
And wail the deed that yet for me remains
To bring to pass; for I will slay my children,
Yea, mine: no man shall pluck them from mine hand.
Then, having brought all Jason's house to wrack,
I leave the land, fleeing my dear babes' blood,
And having dared a deed most impious.
For unendurable are mocks of foes.
Let all go: what is life to me? Nor country
Nor home have I, nor refuge from mine ills.
Then erred I, in the day when I forsook
My father's halls, by yon Greek's words beguiled,
Who with God's help shall render me requital.
For never living shall he see henceforth
The sons I bare him, nor shall he beget
A son of his new bride, that wretch foredoomed
In agony to die by drugs of mine.
Let none account me impotent, nor weak,
Nor spiritless!—O nay, in other sort,
Grim to my foes, and kindly to my friends.
Most glorious is the life of such as I.

CHORUS

Since thou hast made me partner of this tale,—
Wishing to help thee, and yet championing
The laws of men, I say, do thou not this!

MEDEA

It cannot be but so: yet reason is
That thou say this, who art not wronged as I.

CHORUS

Woman, wilt have the heart to slay thy sons?

MEDEA

Yea: so mine husband's heart shall most be wrung.

CHORUS

But thou of wives most wretched shouldst become.

MEDEA

So be it: wasted are all hindering words.
But ho! [*enter* NURSE] go thou and Jason bring to me—
Thou whom I use for every deed of trust,
And look thou tell none aught of mine intent,
If thine is loyal service, thou a woman.

[*Exeunt* MEDEA *and* NURSE.

CHORUS

O happy the race in the ages olden
 Of Erechtheus, the seed of the blest God's line,
In a land unravaged, peace-enfolden,
 Aye quaffing of Wisdom's glorious wine,
Ever through air clear-shining brightly
As on wings uplifted pacing lightly,
Where Harmonia, they tell, of the tresses golden,
 Bare the Pierid Muses, the stainless Nine.[1]

And the streams of Cephisus the lovely-flowing
 They tell how the Lady of Cyprus drew,
And in Zephyr-wafts of the winds sweet-blowing
 Breathed over Attica's land their dew.

---

[1] Another interpretation is equally admitted by the Greek—"Grew, sown by the Muses, the stainless Nine."

On her sons shedding Love which, throned in glory
By Wisdom, shapes her heroic story;
And over her hair is she throwing, throwing,
   Roses in odorous wreaths aye new.

Re-enter MEDEA.

How then should the hallowed city,
   The city of sacred waters,
      Which shields with her guardian hand
      All friends that would fare through her land,
      Receive a murderess banned,
Who had slaughtered her babes without pity,
   A pollution amidst of her daughters?

In thine heart's thoughts set it before thee—
   To murder the fruit of thy womb!
      O think what it meaneth to slay
      Thy sons—what a deed this day
      Thou wouldst do! By thy knees we pray,
By heaven and earth we implore thee,
   Deal not to thy babes such a doom!

O whence, and O whence wilt thou gain thee
   Such desperate hardihood
      That for spirit so fiendish shall serve,
      That shall strengthen thine heart, that shall nerve
      Thine hand, that it shall not swerve
From the ruthless deed that shall stain thee
   With horror of children's blood?

O how, when thine eyes thou art turning
   On thy little ones, wilt thou refrain
      The motherhood in thee, to feel
      No upwelling of tears? Canst thou steel
      Thy breast when thy children kneel,

To crimson thine hand, with unyearning
    Heart for thy darlings slain?
Enter JASON

JASON

I at thy bidding come: albeit my foe,
This grace thou shalt not miss; but I will hear
What new thing, lady, thou dost wish of me.

MEDEA

Jason, I ask thee to forgive the words
Late-spoken. Well thou mayest gently bear
With my wild mood, for all the old love's sake.
Now have I called myself to account, and railed
Upon myself—"Wretch, wherefore am I mad?
And wherefore rage against good counsellors,
And am at feud with rulers of the land,
And with my lord, who works my veriest good,
Wedding a royal house, to raise up brethren
Unto my sons? Shall I not cease from wrath?
What aileth me, when the Gods proffer boons?
Have I not children? Know I not that we
Are exiles from our own land, lacking friends?"
Thus musing, was I ware that I had nursed
Folly exceeding, anger without cause.
Now then I praise thee: wise thou seem'st to me
In gaining us this kinship, senseless I,
Who in these counsels should have been thine ally,
Have furthered all, have decked the bridal couch,
And joyed to minister unto the bride.
But we are—women: needs not harsher word.
Yet shouldst thou not for evil render evil,
Nor pit against my folly folly of thine.

I yield, confessing mine unwisdom then,
But unto better counsels now am come.
Children, my children, hither: leave the house;

[*Enter* CHILDREN.

Come forth, salute your father, and with me
Bid him farewell: be reconciled to friends
Ye, with your mother, from the hate o'erpast.
Truce is between us, rancour hath given place.
Clasp ye his right hand. Woe for ambushed ills
I am haunted by the shadow of hidden things!
Ah children, will ye thus, through many a year
Living, still reach him loving arms? Ah me,
How weeping-ripe am I, how full of fear!
Feuds with your father ended—ah, so late!—
Have filled with tears these soft-relenting eyes.

CHORUS

And from mine eyes start tears of pale dismay.
Ah, may no evil worse than this befall!

JASON

Lady, I praise this mood, yet blame not that:
'Tis nothing strange that womankind should rage
When the spouse trafficketh in alien marriage.
But now to better thoughts thine heart hath turned
And thou, though late, hast seen which policy
Must win: a prudent woman's part is this.
And for you, children, not unheedfully
Your sire hath ta'en much forethought, so help heaven.
For ye, I ween, in this Corinthian land
Shall with your brethren stand the foremost yet.
Grow ye in strength: the rest shall by your sire,
And whatso God is gracious, be wrought out.

You may I see to goodly stature grown,
In manhood's prime, triumphant o'er my foes.
Thou, why with wan tears thus bedew thine eyes,
Turning away from them thy pallid cheek?
Why hear'st thou not with gladness this my speech?

MEDEA

'Tis naught; but o'er these children broods mine heart.

JASON

Fear not: all will I order well for them.

MEDEA

I will be brave—will not mistrust thy words;
But woman is but woman—born for tears.

JASON

Why, hapless one, dost thou sigh over these?

MEDEA

I bare them. When thou prayedst life for them,
Pity stole o'er me, whispering, "Shall this be?"
But that for which thou cam'st to speech of me
In part is said; to speak the rest is mine:
Since the king pleaseth forth the land to send me,—
Yea, for me too 'tis best, I know it well,
That I bide not, a stumblingblock to thee
And the land's lords, whose house's foe I seem,—
Lo, from this land I fare to exile forth:
But, that my sons by thine hand may be reared,
Entreat thou Creon that they be not banished.

JASON

Prevail I may not, yet must I essay.

MEDEA

Nay then, thy bride bid thou to pray her sire
That thy sons be not banished from this land.

JASON

Yea surely; and, I trow, her shall I win.

MEDEA

If of her sister women she is one.
I too will bear a part in thine endeavour;
For I will send her gifts outrivalling far
In beauty aught in these days seen, I know,
A robe fine-spun, a golden diadem;
Our sons to bear them. Now must an attendant
With all speed hither bring the ornaments.
                              [*Handmaid goes,*
Blessings shall hers be, not one, but untold,
Who winneth thee for lord, a peerless spouse,
Who owneth ornaments which once the Sun,
My father's father, to his offspring gave!

Enter handmaid with casket.

Take in your hands, my sons, these bridal gifts,
And to the happy princess-bride bear ye
And give—my gifts she shall not lightly esteem!

JASON

But, fond one, why make void thine hands of these?
Deem'st thou a royal house hath lack of robes,
Or gold, deem'st thou? Keep these and give them not.
For, if my wife esteems me aught, my wish
Will she prefer to treasures, well I wot.

MEDEA

Nay, speak not so: gifts sway the Gods, they say.
Gold weigheth more with men than countless words.
Hers fortune is; God favoureth now her cause—
Young, and a queen! Life would I give for ransom
Of my sons' banishment, not gold alone.
Now, children, enter ye the halls of wealth.
Unto your sire's new wife, my lady-queen,
Make supplication, pray ye be not exiled,
And give mine ornaments—most importeth this,
That she in her own hands receive my gifts.
Haste ye, and to your mother bring glad tidings
Of good success in that she longs to win.

[*Exeunt* JASON *and* CHILDREN.

CHORUS

Now for the life of the children mine hope hath been
    turned to despairing.
No hope any more! On the slaughterward path even now
    are they faring!
The bride shall receive it, the diadem-garland that beareth
    enfolden
            Doom for the hapless mid glittering sheen:
And to set the adorning of Hades about her tresses golden
            She shall take it her hands between.

For its glamour of beauty, its splendour unearthly, shall
    swiftly persuade her
To bedeck her with robe and with gold-wrought crown:
    she shall soon have arrayed her
In attire as a bride in the presence of phantoms from Hades
    uprisen;

In such dread gin shall her feet be ta'en:
In the weird of death shall the hapless be whelmed, and
from Doom's dark prison
Shall she steal forth never again.

And thou, wretch, bridegroom accurst, who art fain of a
princely alliance,
Blasting thou bringest—unknowing, unthink-
ing!—
Of life on thy sons, and thy bride shall to foul death plight
her affiance.
How far from thy fortune of old art thou sinking!

And amidst my lamentings I mourn for thine anguish, O
hapless mother
Of children, who makest thee ready to slaughter
Thy babes, to avenge thee on him who would lawlessly
wed with another,
Would forsake thee to dwell with a prince's
daughter.

Enter CHILDREN'S GUARDIAN, *with* CHILDREN.

CHILDREN'S GUARDIAN

Mistress, remission for thy sons of exile!
Thy gifts the princess-bride with joy received
In hand; and there is peace unto thy sons.
Ha!
Why dost thou stand confounded mid good hap?
Now wherefore turnest thou thy face away,
And dost not hear with gladness this my speech?

MEDEA

Woe's me!

CHILDREN'S GUARDIAN

This cry is to the tidings not attuned.

MEDEA

Woe yet again!

CHILDREN'S GUARDIAN

Can I have brought ill hap
Unwitting—erred in deeming these glad tidings?

MEDEA

As they are, are thy tidings: thee I blame not.

CHILDREN'S GUARDIAN

Why down-drooped is thine eye? Why flow thy tears?

MEDEA

Needs must they, ancient; or these things the Gods
And I withal—O fool!—have ill contrived.

CHILDREN'S GUARDIAN

Fear not: thy children yet shall bring thee home.

MEDEA

Others ere then shall I send home—ah me!

CHILDREN'S GUARDIAN

Not thou alone art severed from thy sons.
Submissively must mortals bear mischance.

MEDEA

This will I: but within the house go thou,

And for my children's daily needs prepare.
[*Exit* CHILDREN'S GUARDIAN.
O children, children, yours a city is,
And yours a home, where, leaving wretched me,
Ye shall abide, for ever motherless!
I shall go exiled to another land,
Ere I have joyed in you, have seen your bliss,
Ere I have decked for you the couch, the bride,
The bridal bower, and held the torch on high.
O me accurst in this my desperate mood!
For naught, for naught, my babes, I nurtured you,
And all for naught I laboured, travail-worn,
Bearing sharp anguish in your hour of birth.
Ah for the hopes—unhappy!—all mine hopes
Of ministering hands about mine age,
Of dying folded round with loving arms,
All men's desire! But now—'tis past—'tis past,
That sweet imagining! Forlorn of you
A bitter life and woeful shall I waste.
Your mother never more with loving eyes
Shall ye behold, passed to another life.
Woe! woe! why gaze your eyes on me, my darlings?
Why smile to me the latest smile of all?
Alas! what shall I do? Mine heart is failing
As I behold the light in my sons' eyes!
Women, I cannot! farewell, purposes
O'erpast! I take my children from the land.
What need to wring their father's heart with ills
Of these, to gain myself ills twice so many?
Not I, not I! Ye purposes, farewell!
Yet—yet—what ails me? Would I earn derision,
Letting my foes slip from mine hand unpunished?
I must dare this. Out on my coward mood

That let words of relenting touch mine heart!
Children, pass ye within.

> [*Exeunt* CHILDREN.
>
> Now, whoso may not

Sinless be present at my sacrifice,
On his head be it: mine hand faltereth not.
Oh! oh!
O heart, mine heart, do not—do not this deed!
Let them be, wretched heart, spare thou my babes!
There dwelling with me shall they gladden thee.
No!—by the nether fiends that dwell with Hades,
Never shall this betide, that I will leave
My children for my foes to trample on!
They needs must die. And, since it needs must be,
Even I will slay them, I, who gave them life.
All this is utter doom:—she shall not 'scape!
Yea, on her head the wreath is; in my robes
The princess-bride is perishing—I know it!
But—for I fare on journey most unhappy,
And shall speed these on yet unhappier—
I would speak to my sons.

> [*Re-enter* CHILDREN.
>
> Give, O my babies,

Give to your mother the right hand to kiss.
O dearest hand, O lips most dear to me,
O form and noble feature of my children,
Blessing be on you—*there!*—for all things here
Your sire hath stolen. Sweet, O sweet embrace!
O children's roseleaf skin, O balmy breath!
Away, away! Strength faileth me to gaze
On you, but I am overcome of evil.

> [*Exeunt* CHILDREN.

Now, now, I learn what horrors I intend:

But passion overmastereth sober thought;
And this is cause of direst ills to men.

CHORUS

I

Full oft ere this my soul hath scaled
  Lone heights of thought, empyreal steeps,
  Or plunged far down the darkling deeps,
Where woman's feebler heart hath failed:—

Yet wherefore failed? Should woman find
  No inspiration thrill her breast,
  Nor welcome ever that sweet guest
Of Song, that uttereth Wisdom's mind?

Alas! not all! Few, a few are they,—
  Perchance amid a thousand one
  Thou shouldest find,—for whom the sun
Of poesy makes an inner day.

II

Now this I say—calm bliss, that ne'er
  Knew love's wild fever of the blood,
  The pains, the joys, of motherhood,
Passeth all parents' joy-blent care.

The childless, they that never prove
  If sunshine comes, or cloud, to men
  With babes—far lie beyond their ken
The toils, the griefs, of parent-love.

But they whose halls with flowerets sweet
  Of childhood bloom—I mark them aye
  Care-fretted, travailing alway
To win their loved ones nurture meet.

III

One toils with love more strong than death:
  Yet—yet—who knoweth whether he
  A wise man or a fool shall be
To whom he shall his wealth bequeath?

But last, but worst, remains to tell:
  For though ye get you wealth enow,
  And though your sons to manhood grow,
Fair sons and good:—if Death the fell,

To Hades vanishing, bears down
  Your children's lives, what profit is
  That Heaven hath laid, with all else, this
Upon mankind, lone sorrow's crown?

MEDEA

Friends, long have I, abiding fortune's hap,
Expected what from yonder shall befall.
And lo, a man I see of Jason's train
Hitherward coming: his wild-fluttering breath
Proclaimeth him the herald of strange ills.
Enter MESSENGER.

MESSENGER

O thou who hast wrought an awful deed and lawless,
Flee, O Medea, flee, nor once leave thou
The sea-wain, or the car that scours the plain.

MEDEA

Now what hath happed that calleth for such flight?

MESSENGER

Dead is the princess even now, and dead
Creon her father, by thy poison-drugs.

MEDEA

A glorious tale thou tellest: thou henceforth
Art of my benefactors and my friends.

MESSENGER

What say'st? Of sound mind art thou, and not mad,
Who, hearing of the havoc of the hearth
Of kings, art glad, and hast no fear for this?

MEDEA

O yea: I too with words of controversy
Could answer thee:—yet be not hasty, friend,
But tell how died they: thou shouldst gladden me
Doubly, if these most horribly have perished.

MESSENGER

When, with their father, came thy children twain,
And passed into the halls for marriage decked,
Glad were we thralls who sorrowed for thy woes;
And straightway buzzed from ear to ear the tale
Of truce to old feuds 'twixt thy lord and thee.
One kissed the hand, and one the golden head
Of those thy sons: myself by joy drawn on
Followed thy children to the women's bowers.
Now she which had our worship in thy stead,
Ere she beheld thy chariot-yoke of sons,
Aye upon Jason turned her yearning gaze.
But then before her eyes she cast her veil,

And swept aback the scorn of her white neck,
Loathing thy sons' approach; but now thy lord,
To turn the maiden's wrath and spite aside,
Thus spake: "Nay, be not hostile to thy friends:
Cease from thine anger, turn thine head again,
Accounting friends whomso thy spouse accounts.
Their gifts receive, and plead thou with thy sire
To pardon these their exile—for my sake."
She, when she saw the attire, could not refrain,
But yielded her lord all. And ere their father
Far from her bower with those thy sons had gone,
She took the rich-wrought robes and clad herself,
Circling her ringlets with the golden crown,
And by a shining mirror ranged her tresses,
Smiling at her own phantom image there.
Then, rising from her seat, adown the halls
She paced with mincing tread of ivory feet,
Exulting in the gifts, and oftentimes
Sweeping her glance from neck to ankle-hem.
But then was there a fearful sight to see.
Suddenly changed her colour: reeling back
With trembling limbs she goes; and scarce in time
Drops on the couch to fall not on the ground.

Then a grey handmaid, deeming peradventure
That frenzy was of Pan or some God sent,
Raised the prayer-cry, before she saw the foam
White-frothing from her lips, or marked how rolled
Her eyeballs, and her face's bloodless hue;
Then a long cry of horror, not of prayer,
She shrilled forth. Straight to her father's chambers **one**
Darted, and one unto her new-made spouse,
To tell the bride's affliction: all the roof

Echoed with multitudinous-hurrying feet.
And a swift athlete's straining limbs had paced
By this the full length of the furlong course,
When she from trance all speechless of closed eyes
In anguish woke with horrible-shrilling shriek;
For like two charging hosts her torment came:—
The golden coil about her head that lay
'Gan spurt a marvellous stream of ravening fire:
The delicate robes, the gift thy children brought,
Had fangs to gnaw her delicate tortured flesh!
Upstarting from her seat she flees, all flame,
Shaking her hair, her head, this way and that,
To cast from her the crown; but firmly fixed
The gold held fast its grip: the fire, whene'er
She shook her locks, with doubled fury blazed.
Then agony-vanquished falls she on the floor,
Marred past all knowledge, save for a father's eyes.
No more was seen her eyes' imperial calm,
No more her comely features; but the gore
Dripped from her head's crown flecked with blended fire.
The flesh-flakes from her bones, like the pine's tears,
'Neath that mysterious drug's devourings melted,—
Dread sight!—and came on all folk fear to touch
The corpse: her hideous fate had we for warning.

But, ignorant of all, her wretched sire,
Suddenly entering, falls upon her corpse,
And straightway wailed and clasped the body round,
And kissed it, crying, "O my hapless child,
What God thus horribly hath thee destroyed?
Who maketh this old sepulchre bereft
Of thee? Ah me, would I might die with thee!"
But when from wailing and from moans he ceased,

Fain would he have upraised his aged frame,
Yet clave, as ivy clings to laurel boughs.
To the filmy robes: then was a ghastly wrestling;
For, while he strained to upraise his knee, she seemed
To upwrithe and grip him: if by force he haled,
Torn from the very bones was his old flesh.
Life's light at last quenched, he gave up the ghost,
Ill-starred, down-sinking 'neath destruction's sea.
There lie the corpses, child by grey old sire
Clasped;—such affliction tears, not words, must mourn.
And of thy part no words be said by me:—
Thyself from punishment wilt find escape.
But man's lot now, as oft, I count a shadow,
Nor fear to say that such as seem to be
In wit most keen of men, most subtle of speech,
Even these pay heaviest penalty of all;
For among mortals happy man is none.
In fortune's flood-tide might a man become
More prosperous than his neighbour; happy?—no!

[*Exit.*

CHORUS

Fortune, meseems, with many an ill this day
Doth compass Jason,—yea, and rightfully.
But O the pity of thy calamity,
Daughter of Creon, who to Hades' halls
Hast passed, because with thee would Jason wed!

MEDEA

Friends, my resolve is taken, with all speed
To slay my children, and to flee this land,
And not to linger and to yield my sons
To death by other hands more merciless.

They needs must die: and, since it needs must be,
Even I will give them death, who gave them life.
Up, gird thee for the fray, mine heart! Why loiter
To do the dread ill deeds that must be done?
Come, wretched hand of mine, grasp thou the sword;
Grasp!—on to the starting-point of a blasted life!
Oh, turn not craven!—think not on thy babes,
How dear they are, how thou didst bear them: nay,
For this short day do thou forget thy sons,
Thereafter mourn them. For, although thou slay,
Yet dear they are, and I—am wretched, wretched!

[*Exit* MEDEA.

CHORUS

O Earth, O all-revealing splendour
  Of the Sun, look down on a woman accurst,
  Or ever she slake the murder-thirst
Of a mother whose hands would smite the tender
      Fruit of her womb.
Look down, for she sprang of thy lineage golden:
Man's vengeance threatens—thy seed are holden
    'Neath the shadow of doom!
But thou, O heaven-begotten glory,
Restrain her, refrain her: the wretched, the gory
Erinys by demons dogged, we implore thee,
    Snatch thou from yon home!

For naught was the childbirth-travail wasted;
  For naught didst thou bear them, the near and the
    dear,
  O thou who hast fled through the Pass of Fear,
From the dark-blue Clashing Crags who hast hasted
    Speeding thy flight!

Alas for her!—wherefore hath grim wrath stirred her
Through depths of her soul, that ruthless murder
   Her wrongs must requite?
For stern upon mortals the vengeance falleth
For kin's blood spilt; from the earth it calleth,
A voice from the Gods, and the slayers appalleth
   On whose homes it shall light.

[CHILDREN's *cries behind the scenes*]

CHILD I

What shall I do?—how flee my mother's hands?

CHILD 2

I know not, dearest brother. Death is here!

CHORUS

Ah the cry!—dost thou hear it?—the children's cry!
Wretch!—woman of cursèd destiny!
Shall I enter? My heart crieth, "Rescue the children from
 murder nigh!"

     [*They beat at the barred doors.*

CHILD I

Help!—for the Gods' sake help! Sore is our need!

CHILD 2

The sword's death-net is closing round us now!
[*Silence within. Blood flows out beneath the door. The
 women shrink back.*]

CHORUS

Wretch! of what rock is thy breast?—of what steel is the
 heart of thee moulded,

That the babes thou hast borne, with the selfsame hands
  that with love have enfolded
      These, thou hast set thee to slay?
Of one have I heard that laid hands on her loved ones of
  old, one only,
Even Ino distraught of the Gods, when Zeus' bride drave
  her, lonely
      And lost, from her home to stray;
      And she fell—ah wretch!—on the brink as she stood
      Of the sea-scaur: guilt of children's blood
      Dragged downwards her feet to the salt sea-flood,
          And she died with her children twain.
      What ghastlier horror remains to be wrought?
      O bride-bed of women, with anguish fraught,
      What scathe upon mortals ere now hast thou brought,
          What manifold bane!

Enter JASON, *with* SERVANTS.

JASON

Women, which stand anear unto this roof—
Is she within the halls, she who hath wrought
Dread deeds, Medea, or in flight passed thence?
For either must she hide her 'neath the earth,
Or lift on wings her frame to heaven's far depths,
Or taste the vengeance of a royal house.
How, trusts she, having murdered the land's lords,
Scathless herself from these halls forth to flee?
Yet not for her care I, but for my sons.
Whom she hath wronged shall recompense her wrong:
But I to save my children's life am come,
Lest to my grief the kinsmen of the dead
Avenge on them their mother's impious murder.

CHORUS

Wretch, thou know'st not how deep thou art whelmed in
  woe,
Jason, or thou hadst uttered not such words.

JASON

What now?—and is she fain to slay me too?

CHORUS

Thy sons are dead, slain by the mother's hand.

JASON

Ah me!—what say'st thou?—thou hast killed me, woman!

CHORUS

Thy children are no more: so think of them.

JASON

How?—slew them? Where?—within, without, the halls?

CHORUS (*pointing to pavement before doors*)

Open, and thou shalt see thy children's corpses.

JASON

Burst in the bolts with all speed, serving-men—
Force hinges!—let me see this twofold horror,—
The dead, and her,—and in her blood avenge me!
  MEDEA *appears above the palace roof in a chariot
        drawn by dragons.*

MEDEA

Why shakest thou these doors and wouldst unbar,
Seeking thy dead and me who wrought the deed?
Cease this essay. If thou wouldst aught of me,

Say what thou wilt: thine hand shall touch me never.
Such chariot hath my father's sire, the Sun,
Given me, a defence from foeman's hand.

JASON

O thing abhorred! O woman hatefullest
To Gods, to me, to all the race of men,
Thou that couldst thrust the sword into the babes
Thou bar'st, and me hast made a childless ruin!
Thus hast thou wrought, yet look'st thou on the sun
And earth, who hast dared a deed most impious?
Now ruin seize thee!—clear I see, who saw not
Then, when from halls and land barbarian
To a Greek home I bare thee, utter bane,
Traitress to sire and land that nurtured thee!
Thy guilt's curse-bolt on me the Gods have launched;
For thine own brother by his heart thou slewest
Ere thou didst enter fair-prowed Argo's hull.
With such deeds thou begannest. Wedded then
To this man, and the mother of my sons,
For wedlock-right's sake hast thou murdered them.
There is no Grecian woman that had dared
This:—yet I stooped to marry thee, good sooth,
Rather than these, a hateful bride and fell,
A tigress, not a woman, harbouring
A fiercer nature than Tyrrhenian Scylla.
But—for untold revilings would not sting
Thee, in thy nature is such hardihood:—
Avaunt, thou miscreant stained with thy babes' blood!
For me remains to wail my destiny,
Who of my new-wed bride shall have no joy,
And to the sons whom I begat and nurtured
Living I shall not speak—lost, lost to me!

MEDEA

I might have lengthened out long controversy
To these thy words, if Father Zeus knew not
How I have dealt with thee and thou with me.
'Twas not for thee to set my rights at naught,
And live a life of bliss, bemocking me,
Nor for thy princess, and thy marriage-kinsman,
Creon, unscathed to banish me this land!
Wherefore a tigress call me, an thou wilt,
Or Scylla, haunter of Tyrrhenian shore;
For thine heart have I wrung, as well behoved.

JASON

Ha, but thou sorrowest too, dost share mine ills!

MEDEA

O yea: yet grief is gain, so thou laugh not.

JASON

O children mine, what miscreant mother had ye!

MEDEA

O sons, destroyed by your own father's lust!

JASON

Sooth, 'twas no hand of mine that murdered them.

MEDEA

Nay, but thine insolence and thy new-forged bonds.

JASON

How, claim the right for wedlock's sake to slay them!

MEDEA

A light affliction count'st thou this to a wife?

JASON

A virtuous wife:—in *thy* sight naught were good!

MEDEA

These live no more: this, this shall cut thine heart!

JASON

They live—ah me!—avengers on thine head.

MEDEA

The Gods know who began this misery.

JASON

Yea, verily, thy spirit abhorred they know.

MEDEA

Abhorred art thou: I loathe thy bitter tongue.

JASON

And I thine:—yet were mutual riddance easy.

MEDEA

How then?—what shall I do?—fain would I this.

JASON

Yield me my dead to bury and bewail.

MEDEA

Never: with this hand will I bury them,

To Mountain Hera's precinct bearing them,
That never foe may do despite to them,
Rifling their tomb. This land of Sisyphus
Will I constrain with solemn festival
And rites to atone for this unhallowed murder.
But I—I go unto Erechtheus' land,
With Aegeus to abide, Pandion's son.
Thou, as is meet, foul wretch, shalt foully die,
By Argo's wreckage smitten on the skull,
Who hast seen this new bridal's bitter ending.

JASON

Now the Fury-avenger of children smite thee,
And Justice that looketh on murder requite thee!

MEDEA

What God or what spirit will heed thy request,
Caitiff forsworn, who betrayest the guest?

JASON

Avaunt, foul thing by whose deed thy children have died!

MEDEA

Go hence to thine halls, thence lead to the grave thy bride!

JASON

I go, a father forlorn of the two sons reft from his home!

MEDEA

Not yet dost thou truly mourn: abide till thine old age come.

JASON

O children beloved above all!

MEDEA

Of their mother beloved, not of thee.

JASON

Yet she slew them!

MEDEA

That thou mightest fall in the net that
thou spreadest for me.

JASON

Woe's me! I yearn with my lips to press
My sons' dear lips in my wretchedness.

MEDEA

Ha, now art thou calling upon them, now wouldst thou
kiss,
Who rejectedst them then?

JASON

For the Gods' sake grant me but this,
The sweet soft flesh of my children to feel!

MEDEA

No—wasted in air is all thine appeal.

JASON

O Zeus, dost thou hear it, how spurned I am?—
What courage I suffer of yonder abhorred
Child-murderess, yonder tigress-dam?
Yet out of mine helplessness, out of my shame,
I bewail my belovèd, I call to record
High heaven, I bid God witness the word,

That my sons thou hast slain, and withholdest me,
That mine hands may not touch them, nor bury their
 clay!
Would God I had gotten them never, this day
 To behold them destroyed of thee!

CHORUS

All dooms be of Zeus in Olympus; 'tis his to reveal them.
 Manifold things unhoped-for the Gods to accomplish-
  ment bring.
And the things that we looked for, the Gods deign not to
 fulfil them;
And the paths undiscerned of our eyes, the Gods unseal
 them.
  So fell this marvellous thing.

        [Exeunt OMNES.

THE FROGS

BY

ARISTOPHANES

DRAMATIS PERSONÆ

BACCHUS.
XANTHIAS, *servant of Bacchus*.
HERCULES.
CHARON.
ÆACUS.
EURIPIDES.
ÆSCHYLUS.
PLUTO.
DEAD MAN.
PROSERPINE'S SERVANT MAID.
TWO WOMEN SUTLERS.
MUTES.
CHORUS OF VOTARIES, *and*
FROGS.

THE ARGUMENT

BACCHUS, the patron of the stage, in despair at the decline of the dramatic art (which had lately been deprived of its best tragic authors, Sophocles and Euripides), determines to descend the infernal regions with the intention of procuring the release of Euripides. He appears accordingly, equipped for the expedition, with the lion's skin and club (in imitation of Hercules, whose success in a similar adventure has encouraged him to the attempt); he still retains, however, his usual effeminate costume, which forms a contrast with these heroic attributes. Xanthias, his slave (like Silenus, the mythologic attendant of Bacchus), is mounted upon an ass; but in conformity with the practice of other human slaves when attending their mortal masters upon an earthly journey, he carries a certain pole upon his shoulder, at the ends of which the various packages, necessary for his master's accommodation, are suspended in equilibrio. The first scene (which, if it had not been the first, might perhaps have been omitted) contains a censure of the gross taste of the audience (suitable to the character of Bacchus as patron of the stage) with allusions to some contemporary rival authors, who submitted to court the applause of the vulgar by mere buffoonery.—The argument between Bacchus and Xanthias, at the end of this scene, probably contains some temporary allusion now unknown, but is obviously, and in the first place, a humorous exemplification of the philosophical, verbal sophisms, not, in all probability, new, even then, but which were then, for the first time, introduced in Athens, and which may be traced from thence to the schoolmen of the middle ages. Xanthias carries the bundles *passivè* et *formaliter,* the ass carries them *activè* et *materialiter.*

THE FROGS

BACCHUS. XANTHIAS.

Xan. Master, shall I begin with the usual jokes
  That the audience always laugh at?
Bac.   If you please;
  Any joke you please except "being overburthen'd."
  —Don't use it yet—We've time enough before us.
Xan. Well, something else that's comical and clever?
Bac. I forbid being "overpress'd and overburthen'd."
Xan. Well, but the drollest joke of all—?
Bac.   Remember
  There's one thing I .protest against—
Xan.   What's that?
Bac. Why, shifting off your load to the other shoulder,
  And fidgeting and complaining of the gripes.
Xan. What then do you mean to say, that I must not say
  That I'm ready to befoul myself?
Bac. (peremptorily).   By no means
  Except when I take an emetic.
*Xan. (in a sullen, muttering tone, as if resentful of hard
    usage)*
                                   What's the use, then,
  Of my being burthen'd here with all these bundles.
  If I'm to be deprived of the common jokes
  That Phrynichus, and Lycis, and Ameipsias
  Allow the servants always in their comedies,
  Without exception, when they carry bundles?

Bac. Pray, leave them off—for those ingenious sallies
 Have such an effect upon my health and spirits
 That I feel grown old and dull when I get home.
Xan. (*as before, or with a sort of half-mutinous whine*).
 It's hard for me to suffer in my limbs,
 To be overburthen'd and debarr'd from joking.
Bac. Well, this is monstrous, quite, and insupportable!
 Such insolence in a servant! When your master
 Is going afoot and has provided you
 With a beast to carry ye.
Xan.   What! do I carry nothing?
Bac. You're carried yourself.
Xan.   But I carry bundles, don't I?
Bac. But the beast bears all the burdens that you carry.
Xan. Not those that I carry myself—'tis I that carry 'em.
Bac. You're carried yourself, I tell ye.
Xan.   I can't explain it,
 But I feel it in my shoulders plainly enough.
Bac. Well, if the beast don't help you, take and try;
 Change places with the ass and carry him.
Xan. (*in a tone of mere disgust*).
 Oh, dear! I wish I had gone for a volunteer,
 And left you to yourself. I wish I had.
Bac. Dismount, you rascal! Here, we're at the house
 Where Hercules lives.—Holloh! there! who's within
 there?

       [*Bacchus kicks outrageously at the door.*

    HERCULES. BACCHUS. XANTHIAS.

Her. Who's there? (He has bang'd at the door, whoever
 he is,
 With the kick of a centaur.) What's the matter, there?
Bac. (*aside*). Ha! Xanthias!

Xan. What?

Bac. (*aside*). Did ye mind how he was frighten'd?

Xan. I suppose he was afraid you were going mad.

Her. (*aside*). By Jove! I shall laugh outright; I'm ready to burst.

I shall laugh, in spite of myself, upon my life.

> [*Hercules shifts about, and turns aside to disguise his laughter: this apparent shyness confirms Bacchus in the opinion of his own ascendancy, which he manifests accordingly.*

Bac. (*with a tone of protection*).

Come hither, friend.—What ails ye? Step this way;
I want to speak to ye.

Her. (*with a good-humoured, but unsuccessful endeavour to suppress laughter, or to conceal it. Suppose him, for instance, speaking with his hand before his mouth*).

But I can't help laughing,
To see the lion's skin with a saffron robe,
And the club with the women's sandals—altogether—
What's the meaning of it all? Have you been abroad?

Bac. I've been abroad—in the Fleet—with Cleisthenes.

Her. (*sharply and ironically*). You fought—?

Bac. (*briskly and sillily*). Yes, that we did—we gain'd a victory;

And we sunk the enemies' ships—thirteen of 'em.

Her. "So you woke at last and found it was a dream?"

Bac. But aboard the fleet, as I pursued my studies,
I read the tragedy of Andromeda;
And then such a vehement passion struck my heart,
You can't imagine.

Her. A small one, I suppose,
My little fellow—a moderate little passion?

Bac. (*ironically: the irony of imbecility*).

It's just as small as Molon is—that's all—
Molon the wrestler, I mean—as small as he is—

Her. Well, what was it like? what kind of a thing? what
was it?

Bac. (*meaning to be very serious and interesting*).
No, friend, you must not laugh; it's past a joke;
It's quite a serious feeling—quite distressing;
I suffer from it—

Her. (*bluntly*). Well, explain. What was it?

Bac. I can't declare it at once; but I'll explain it
Theatrically and enigmatically:

> [*With a buffoonish assumption of tragic gesture
> and emphasis.*

Were you ever seized with a sudden passionate longing
For a mess of porridge?

Her.   Often enough, if that's all.

Bac. Shall I state the matter to you plainly at once;
Or put it circumlocutorily?

Her. Not about the porridge. I understand your instance.

Bac. Such is the passion that possesses me
For poor Euripides, that's dead and gone;
And it's all in vain people trying to persuade me
From going after him.

Her.   What, to the shades below?

Bac. Yes, to the shades below, or the shades beneath 'em.
To the undermost shades of all. I'm quite determined.

Her. But what's your object?

Bac. (*with a ridiculous imitation of tragical action and
emphasis*).

                          Why my object is
That I want a clever poet—"for the good,
The gracious and the good, are dead and gone;
The worthless and the weak are left alive."

Her. Is not Iophon a good one?—He's alive sure?
Bac. If he's a good one, he's our only good one;
 But it's a question; I'm in doubt about him.
Her. There's Sophocles; he's older than Euripides—
 If you go so far for 'em, you'd best bring him.
Bac. No; first I'll try what Iophon can do,
 Without his father, Sophocles, to assist him.
 —Besides, Euripides is a clever rascal;
 A sharp, contriving rogue that will make a shift
 To desert and steal away with me; the other
 Is an easy-minded soul, and always was.
Her. Where's Agathon?
Bac. He's gone and left me too,
 Regretted by his friends; a worthy poet—
Her. Gone! Where, poor soul?
Bac. To the banquets of the blest!
Her. But then you've Xenocles—
Bac. Yes! a plague upon him!
Her. Pythangelus too—
Xan. But nobody thinks of me;
 Standing all this while with the bundles on my shoulder.
Her. But have not you other young ingenious youths
 That are fit to out-talk Euripides ten times over;
 To the amount of a thousand, at least, all writing
 tragedy—?
Bac. They're good for nothing—"Warblers of the Grove"—
 —"Little, foolish, fluttering things"—poor puny wretches,
 That dawdle and dangle about with the tragic muse;
 Incapable of any serious meaning—
 —There's not one hearty poet amongst them all
 That's fit to risk an adventurous valiant phrase.
Her. How—"hearty?" What do you mean by "valiant
 phrases?"

Bac. (*the puzzle of a person who is called upon for a definition*).

    I mean a . . . kind . . . of a . . . doubtful, bold expression
To talk about . . . "*The viewless foot of Time*"—
               [*Tragic emphasis in the quotations.*
And . . . "*Jupiter's Secret Chamber in the Skies*"—
And about . . . A person's soul . . . not being perjured
When . . . the tongue . . . forswears itself . . . in spite
    of the soul.

Her. Do you like that kind of stuff?
Bac.   I'm crazy after it.
Her. Why, sure, it's trash and rubbish—Don't you think
    so?
Bac. "Men's fancies are their own—Let mine alone"—
Her. But, in fact, it seems to me quite bad—rank nonsense.
Bac. You'll tell me next what I ought to like for supper.
Xan. But nobody thinks of me here, with the bundles.
Bac. (*with a careless, easy, voluble, degagé style*).

  —But now to the business that I came upon—
       [*Upon a footing of equality.—The tone of a person
          who is dispatching business off-hand, with readi-
          ness and unconcern.*

(With the apparel that you see—the same as yours)
To obtain a direction from you to your friends,
(To apply to them—in case of anything—
If anything should occur) the acquaintances
That received you there—(the time you went before
—For the business about Cerberus)—if you'd give me
Their names and their directions, and communicate
Any information relative to the country,
The roads,—the streets,—the bridges, and the brothels,
The wharfs,—the public walks,—the public houses,
The fountains,—aqueducts,—and inns, and taverns,

And lodgings,—free from bugs and fleas, if possible.
If you know any such—
Xan.   But nobody thinks of me.
Her. What a notion! You! will you risk it? are you mad?
Bac. (*meaning to be very serious and manly*).
  I beseech you say no more—no more of that,
  But inform me briefly and plainly about my journey:
  The shortest road and the most convenient one.
Her. (*with a tone of easy, indolent, deliberate banter*).
  Well,—which shall I tell ye first, now?—Let me see now—
  There's a good convenient road by the Rope and Noose;
  The Hanging Road.
Bac.   No; that's too close and stifling.
Her. Then, there's an easy, fair, well-beaten track,
  As you go by the Pestle and Mortar—
Bac.   What, the Hemlock?
Her. To be sure—
Bac.   That's much too cold—it will never do.
  They tell me it strikes a chill to the legs and feet.
Her. Should you like a speedy, rapid, downhill road?
Bac. Indeed I should, for I'm a sorry traveller.
Her. Go to the Keramicus then.
Bac.   What then?
Her. Get up to the very top of the tower.
Bac.   What then?
Her. Stand there and watch when the Race of the Torch
    begins;
  And mind when you hear the people cry *"Start! start!"*
  Then start at once with 'em.
Bac.   Me? Start? Where from?
Her. From the top of the tower to the bottom.
Bac.   No, not I.

It's enough to dash my brains out! I'll not go
Such a road upon any account.
Her.   Well, which way then?
Bac. The way you went yourself.
Her.   But it's a long one,
For first you come to a monstrous bottomless lake.
Bac. And what must I do to pass?
Her.   You'll find a boat there;
A little tiny boat, as big as that,
And an old man that ferries you over in it,
Receiving twopence as the usual fee.
Bac. Ah! that same twopence governs everything
Wherever it goes.—I wonder how it managed
To find its way there?
Her   Theseus introduced it
—Next you'll meet serpents, and wild beasts, and mon-
    sters,
                    [Suddenly and with a shout in Bacchus's ear.
Horrific to behold!
Bac. (*starting a little*). Don't try to fright me;
You'll not succeed, I promise you.—I'm determined.
Her. Then there's an abyss of mire and floating filth,
In which the damn'd lie wallowing and overwhelm'd;
The unjust, the cruel, and the inhospitable;
And the barbarous bilking Cullies that withhold
The price of intercourse with fraud and wrong;
The incestuous, and the parricides, and the robbers;
The perjurers, and assassins, and the wretches
That wilfully and presumptuously transcribe
Extracts and trash from Morsimus's plays.
Bac. And, by Jove! Cinesias with his Pyrrhic dancers
Ought to be there—they're worse, or quite as bad.
Her. But after this your sense will be saluted

With a gentle breathing sound of flutes and voices,
And a beautiful spreading light like ours on earth,
And myrtle glades and happy quires among,
Of women and men with rapid applause and mirth.
Bac. And who are all those folks?
Her.   The initiated.
Xan. (*gives indications of restiveness, as if ready to throw
        down his bundles*).
I won't stand here like a mule in a procession
Any longer, with these packages and bundles.
Her. (*hastily, in a civil hurry, as when you shake a man by
    the hand, and shove him out of the room, and give him
    your best wishes and advice all at once*).
They'll tell you everything you want to know,
For they're established close upon the road,
By the corner of Pluto's house—so fare you well;
Farewell, my little fellow.   [*Exit.*
Bac. (*pettishly*).   I wish you better.
(*to Xanthias*) You, sirrah, take your bundles up again.
Xan. What, before I put them down?
Bac.   Yes! now, this moment.
Xan. Nah! don't insist; there's plenty of people going
As corpses with the convenience of a carriage;
They'd take it for a trifle gladly enough.
Bac. But if we meet with nobody?
Xan.   Then I'll take 'em.
Bac. Come, come, that's fairly spoken, and in good time:
For there they're carrying a corpse out to be buried.
        [*A funeral, with a corpse on an open bier, crosses
            the stage.*
—Holloh! you there—you Deadman—can't you hear?
Would you take any bundles to hell with ye, my good
    fellow?

Deadman.　What are they?

Bac.　　　　　　These.

Deadman.　　　　　　　Then I must have two drachmas.

Bac.　I can't—you must take less.

Deadman (*peremptorily*).　　　Bearers, move on.

Bac.　No, stop! we shall settle between us—you're so hasty.

Deadman.　It's no use arguing; I must have two drachmas.

Bac. (*emphatically and significantly*).　Ninepence!

Deadman.　　　　I'd best be alive again at that rate. [*Exit.*

Bac.　Fine airs the fellow gives himself—a rascal!
　I'll have him punish'd, I vow, for overcharging.

Xan.　Best give him a good beating: give me the bundles,
　I'll carry 'em.

Bac.　　　　　You're a good, true-hearted fellow;
　And a willing servant.—Let's move on to the ferry.

CHARON.　BACCHUS.　XANTHIAS.

Char.　Hoy!　Bear a hand, there—Heave ashore.

Bac.　　　　　　　　　　　What's this?

Xan.　The lake it is—the place he told us of.
　By Jove! and there's the boat—and here's old Charon.

Bac.　Well, Charon! — Welcome, Charon! — Welcome
　kindly!

Char.　Who wants the ferryman?　Anybody waiting
　To remove from the sorrows of life?　A passage anybody?
　To Lethe's wharf?—to Cerberus's Reach?
　To Tartarus?—to Tænarus?—to Perdition?

Bac.　Yes, I.

Char.　　　　Get in then.

Bac. (*hesitatingly*).　　Tell me, where are you going?
　To Perdition really—?

Char. (*not sarcastically, but civilly in the way of business*).
　　　　　　　Yes, to oblige you, I will

With all my heart—Step in there.
Bac.   Have a care!
Take care, good Charon!—Charon, have a care!
                              [*Bacchus gets into the boat.*
Come, Xanthias, come!
Char.   I take no slaves aboard
Except they've volunteer'd for the naval victory.
Xan. I could not—I was suffering with sore eyes.
Char. You must trudge away then, round by the end of
the lake there.
Xan. And whereabouts shall I wait?
Char.   At the Stone of Repentance,
By the Slough of Despond beyond the Tribulations;
You understand me?
Xan.   Yes, I understand you;
A lucky, promising direction, truly.
Char. (*to Bac.*). Sit down at the oar—Come quick, it
there's more coming!
(*To Bac. again*) Holloh! what's that you're doing?
      [*Bacchus is seated in a buffoonish attitude on the
      side of the boat where the oar was fastened.*
Bac...   What you told me.
I'm sitting at the oar.
Char.   Sit there, I tell you,
You Fatguts; that's your place.
Bac. (*changes his place*).   Well, so I do.
Char. Now ply your hands and arms.
Bac. (*makes a silly motion with his arms*). Well, so I do
Char. You'd best leave off your fooling. Take to the oar,
And pull away.
Bac.   But how shall I contrive?
I've never served on board—I'm only a landsman;
I'm quite unused to it—

Char.   We can manage it.
   As soon as you begin you shall have some music
   That will teach you to keep time.
Bac.   What music's that?
Char.   A chorus of Frogs—uncommon musical Frogs.
Bac.   Well, give me the word and the time.
Char.   Whooh up, up; whooh up, up.

CHORUS

   Brekekekex-koax-koax,
   Shall the Choral Quiristers of the Marsh
   Be censured and rejected as hoarse and harsh;
      And their Chromatic essays
      Deprived of praise?
   No, let us raise afresh
   Our obstreperous Brekekekex;
   The customary croak and cry
      Of the creatures
      At the theatres,
   In their yearly revelry,
   Brekekekex-koax-koax.
Bac. (*rowing in great misery*)
   How I'm maul'd,
   How I'm gall'd;
   Worn and mangled to a mash—
   There they go! "*Koax-koax!*"—
Frogs.   Brekekekex-koax-koax.
Bac.   Oh, beshrew,
               All your crew;
   You don't consider how I smart.
Frogs.   Now for a sample of the Art!
        Brekekekex-koax-koax.
Bac.   I wish you hang'd, with all my heart.

—Have you nothing else to say?
"Brekekekex-koax-koax" all day!

Frogs.   We've a right,
We've a right;
And we croak at ye for spite.
We've a right,
We've a right;
Day and night,
Day and night;
Night and day,
Still to Creak and croak away.
Phœbus and every Grace
Admire and approve of the croaking race;
And the egregious guttural notes
That are gargled and warbled in their lyrical throats.
In reproof
Of your scorn
Mighty Pan
Nods his horn;
Beating time
To the rhyme
With his hoof,
With his hoof.
Persisting in our plan,
We proceed as we began,
Brekekekex-brekekekex,
Kooax, kooax.

Bac. Oh, the Frogs, consume and rot 'em,
I've a blister on my bottom.
Hold your tongues, you tuneful creatures.

Frogs. Cease with your profane entreaties
All in vain for ever striving:
Silence is against our natures.

With the vernal heat reviving,
  Our acquatic crew repair
From their periodic sleep,
In the dark and chilly deep,
To the cheerful upper air;
Then we frolic here and there
All amidst the meadows fair;
Shady plants of asphodel,
Are the lodges where we dwell;
Chaunting in the leafy bowers
All the livelong summer hours,
Till the sudden gusty showers
Send us headlong, helter, skelter,
To the pool to seek for shelter;
Meagre, eager, leaping, lunging,
From the sedgy wharfage plunging
To the tranquil depth below,
There we muster all a-row;
Where, secure from toil and trouble,
With a tuneful hubble-bubble,
Our symphonious accents flow.
Brekekekex-koax-koax.

Bac.   I forbid you to proceed.
Frogs. That would be severe indeed;
Arbitrary, bold, and rash—
Brekekekex-koax-koax.
Bac.   I command you to desist—
   —Oh, my back, there! oh, my wrist!
What a twist!
What a sprain!
Frogs. Once again—
We renew the tuneful strain,
Brekekekex-koax-koax.

Bac.   I disdain—(Hang the pain!)
        All your nonsense, noise, and trash.
        Oh, my blister! Oh, my sprain!
Frogs. Brekekekex-koax-koax.
        Friends and Frogs, we must display
        All our powers of voice to-day;
        Suffer not this stranger here,
        With fastidious foreign ear,
        To confound us and abash.
        Brekekekex-koax-koax.
Bac.   Well, my spirit is not broke,
        If it's only for the joke,
        I'll outdo you with a croak.
        Here it goes—(*very loud*) "Koax-koax."
Frogs. Now for a glorious croaking crash, [*Still louder.—*
        Brekekekex-koax-koax.
Bac. (*splashing with his oar*).
        I'll disperse you with a splash.
Frogs. Brekekekex-hoax-hoax.
Bac.   I'll subdue
        Your rebellious, noisy crew—
        —Have amongst you there, slap-dash.
                                    [*Strikes at them.*
Frogs. Brekekekex-koax-koax.
        We defy your oar and you.
Char. Hold! We're ashore just—shift your oar. Get out.
        —Now pay for your fare.
Bac.   There—there it is—the twopence.

CHARON *returns.* BACCHUS, *finding himself alone and in a
        strange place, begins to call out.*

Bac. Hoh, Xanthias! Xanthias, I say! Where's Xanthias?
Xan. A-hoy!

Bac.   Come here.

Xan.   I'm glad to see you, master.

Bac. What's that before us there?

Xan.   The mire and darkness.

Bac. Do you see the villains and the perjurers
  That he told us of?

Xan.   Yes, plain enough, don't you?

Bac. Ah! now I see them, indeed, quite plain—and now
    too.   [*Turning to the audience.*
  Well, what shall we do next?

Xan.   We'd best move forward;
  For here's the place that Hercules there inform'd us
  Was haunted by those monsters.

Bac.   Oh, confound him!
  He vapour'd and talk'd at random to deter me
  From venturing. He's amazingly conceited
  And jealous of other people, is Hercules;
  He reckon'd I should rival him, and, in fact
  (Since I've come here so far), I should rather like
  To meet with an adventure in some shape.

Xan. By Jove! and I think I hear a kind of a noise.

Bac. Where? where?

Xan.   There, just behind us.

Bac.   Go behind, then.

Xan. There!—it's before us now.—There!

Bac.   Go before, then.

Xan. Ah! now I see it—a monstrous beast indeed!

Bac. What kind?

Xan.   A dreadful kind—all kinds at once.
  It changes and transforms itself about
  To a mule and an ox,—and now to a beautiful creature;
  A woman!

Bac.   Where? where is she? Let me seize her.

Xan. But now she's turned to a mastiff all of a sudden.

Bac. It's the Weird hag! the Vampyre!

Xan. (*collectedly*).   Like enough.
She's all of a blaze of fire about the mouth.

Bac. (*with great trepidation*).
Has she got the brazen foot?

Xan. (*with cool despair*).   Yes, there it is—
By Jove!—and the cloven hoof to the other leg,
Distinct enough—that's she!

Bac.   But what shall I do?

Xan. And I, too?

> [*Bacchus runs to the front of the stage, where there
> was a seat of honour appropriated to the priest of
> Bacchus.*

Bac.   Save me, Priest, protect and save me,
That we may drink and be jolly together hereafter.

Xan. We're ruin'd, Master Hercules.

Bac.   Don't call me so, I beg.
Don't mention my name, good friend, upon any account.

Xan. Well, Bacchus, then!

Bac.   That's worse, ten thousand times.

> [*Bacchus remains hiding his face before the seat of
> the priest—in the meantime affairs take a more
> favourable turn.*

Xan. (*cheerfully*).   Come, master, move along—Come,
come this way.

Bac. (*without looking round*).
What's happened?

Xan.   Why we're prosperous and victorious:
The storm of fear and danger has subsided,
And (as the actor said the other day)
"Has only left a gentle *qualm* behind."
The Vampyre's vanish'd.

Bac.   Has she? upon your oath?
Xan.   By Jove! she has.
Bac.   No. swear again.
Xan.   By Jove!
Bac.   Is she, by Jupiter?
Xan.   By Jupiter!
Bac.   Oh dear; what a fright I was in with the very sight
   of her:
   It turn'd me sick and pale—but see, the priest here!
   He has colour'd up quite with the same alarm.
   —What has brought me to this pass?—It must be Jupiter
   With his *"Chamber in the Skies,"* and the *"Foot of Time."*
          [*A flute sounds. Bacchus remains absorbed and
             inattentive to the objects about him.*
Xan.   Holloh, you!
Bac.   What?
Xan.   Why, did you not hear?
Bac.   Why, what?
Xan.   The sound of a flute.
Bac. (*recollecting himself*). Indeed! And there's a smell
   too;
   A pretty mystical ceremonious smell
   Of torches. We'll watch here, and keep quite quiet.

CHORUS OF VOTARIES. BACCHUS. XANTHIAS.

CHORUS.—*Shouting and Singing.*

Iacchus! Iacchus! Ho!
Iacchus! Iacchus! Ho!

Xan.   There, Master, there they are, the initiated;
   All sporting about as he told us we should find 'em.
   They're singing in praise of Bacchus like Diagoras.
Bac.   Indeed, and so they are; but we'll keep quiet
   Till we make them out a little more distinctly.

CHORUS.—*Song.*

Mighty Bacchus! Holy Power!
Hither at the wonted hour
  Come away,
  Come away,
With the wanton holiday,
Where the revel uproar leads
To the mystic holy meads,
Where the frolic votaries fly,
With a tipsy shout and cry;
Flourishing the Thyrsus high,
Flinging forth, alert and airy,
To the sacred old vagary,
The tumultuous dance and song,
Sacred from the vulgar throng;
Mystic orgies, that are known
To the votaries alone—
To the mystic chorus solely—
Secret—unreveal'd—and holy.

Xan. Oh glorious virgin, daughter of the goddess!
What a scent of roasted griskin reach'd my senses.
Bac. Keep quiet—and watch for a chance of a piece of the
haslets.

CHORUS.—*Song.*

Raise the fiery torches high!
Bacchus is approaching nigh,
Like the planet of the morn,
Breaking with the hoary dawn,
  On the dark solemnity—
There they flash upon the sight;
All the plain is blazing bright,
Flush'd and overflown with light:

Age has cast his years away,⎫
And the cares of many a day,⎬
Sporting to the lively lay—⎭
Mighty Bacchus! march and lead
(Torch in hand toward the mead)
Thy devoted humble Chorus,
Mighty Bacchus—move before us!

SEMICHORUS.

Keep silence—keep peace—and let all the profane
From our holy solemnity duly refrain;
Whose souls unenlightened by taste, are obscure;
Whose poetical notions are dark and impure;
  Whose theatrical conscience
  Is sullied by nonsense;
Who never were train'd by the mighty Cratinus
In mystical orgies poetic and vinous;
Who delight in buffooning and jests out of season;
Who promote the designs of oppression and treason;
Who foster sedition, and strife, and debate;
All traitors, in short, to the stage and the state;
Who surrender a fort, or in private, export
To places and harbours of hostile resort,
Clandestine consignments of cables and pitch;
In the way that Thorycion grew to be rich
From a scoundrelly dirty collector of tribute:
All such we reject and severely prohibit:
All statesmen retrenching the fees and the salaries
Of theatrical bards, in revenge for the railleries,
And jests, and lampoons, of this holy solemnity,
Profanely pursuing their personal enmity,
For having been flouted, and scoff'd, and scorn'd,
All such are admonish'd and heartily warn'd;

We warn them once,
We warn them twice,
We warn and admonish—we warn them thrice,
To conform to the law,
To retire and withdraw;   ⎫
While the Chorus again with the formal saw ⎬
(Fixt and assign'd to the festive day)   ⎭
Move to the measure and march away.

SEMICHORUS.

March! march! lead forth,
Lead forth manfully,
March in order all;
Bustling, hustling, justling,
    As it may befall;
    Flocking, shouting, laughing,
Mocking, flouting, quaffing,
    One and all;
All have had a belly-full
Of breakfast brave and plentiful;
    Therefore
    Evermore
With your voices and your bodies
Serve the goddess,
    And raise
    Songs of praise;
She shall save the country still,
    And save it against the traitor's will;
    So she says.

SEMICHORUS.

Now let us raise, in a different strain,
The praise of the goddess to giver of grain;

Imploring her favour
With other behaviour,
In measures more sober, submissive, and graver.

SEMICHORUS.

Ceres, holy patroness,
Condescend to mark and bless
With benevolent regard,
Both the Chorus and the Bard;
Grant them for the present day
Many things to sing and say,
Follies intermix'd with sense;
Folly, but without offence.
Grant them with the present play
To bear the prize of verse away.

SEMICHORUS.

Now call again, and with a different measure,
    The power of mirth and pleasure;
The florid, active Bacchus, bright and gay,
    To journey forth and join us on the way.

SEMICHORUS.

O Bacchus, attend! the customary patron
    Of every lively lay;   ⎫
    Go forth without delay   ⎬
    Thy wonted annual way,   ⎭
To meet the ceremonious holy matron:
    Her grave procession gracing,
    Thine airy footsteps tracing
With unlaborious, light, celestial motion;
And here at thy devotion

Behold thy faithful quire
In pitiful attire;
All overworn and ragged,
This jerkin old and jagged,
These buskins torn and burst,
  Though sufferers in the fray.
May serve us at the worst
  To sport throughout the day;
And there within the shades,
I spy some lovely maids;
With whom we romp'd and revell'd,
Dismantled and dishevell'd;
With their bosoms open,
With whom we might be coping.

Xan. Well, I was always hearty,
Disposed to mirth and ease,
I'm ready to join the party.

Bac. (*with a tone of imbecility, like Sir Andrew Ague-
cheek's "Yes, and I too"—"Ay or I either"*).
And I will, if you please.

BACCHUS (*to the* CHORUS).

Prithee, my good fellows,
Would you please to tell us
  Which is Pluto's door,
I'm an utter stranger,
  Never here before.

CHORUS.

Friend, you're out of danger,
  You need not seek it far;
There it stands before ye,
  Before ye, where you are.

Bac. Take up your bundles, Xanthias.
Xan.   Hang all bundles;
  A bundle has no end, and these have none.
                              [*Exeunt Bacchus and Xanthias.*

SEMICHORUS.

Now we go to dance and sing
  In the consecrated shades;
Round the secret holy ring,
  With the matrons and the maids.
Thither I must haste to bring
  The mysterious early light;
  Which must witness every rite
  Of the joyous happy night.

SEMICHORUS.

Let us hasten—let us fly—
Where the lovely meadows lie;
  Where the living waters flow;
  Where the roses bloom and blow.
—Heirs of Immortality,
Segregated, safe and pure,
Easy, sorrowless, secure;
Since our earthly course is run,
We behold a brighter sun.
Holy lives—a holy vow—
Such rewards await them now.

Scene. The Gate of Pluto's Palace.

Enter BACCHUS *and* XANTHIAS.

Bac. (*going up to the door with considerable hesitation*).
  Well, how must I knock at the door now? Can't ye tell
  me?

How do the native inhabitants knock at doors?

Xan. Pah; don't stand fooling there; but smite it smartly,
With the very spirit and air of Hercules.

Bac. Holloh!

Æacus (from within, with the voice of a royal and infernal porter).

Who's there?

Bac. (with a forced voice). 'Tis I, the valiant Hercules!

Æacus. (coming out).

Thou brutal, abominable, detestable,
Vile, villainous, infamous, nefarious scoundrel!
—How durst thou, villain as thou wert, to seize
Our watch-dog, Cerberus, whom I kept and tended
Hurrying him off, half-strangled in your grasp?
—But now, be sure we have you safe and fast,
Miscreant and villain!—Thee, the Stygian cliffs,
With stern adamantine durance, and the rocks
Of inaccessible Acheron, red with gore,
Environ and beleaguer; and the watch,
And swift pursuit of the hideous hounds of hell;
And the horrible Hydra, with her hundred heads,
Whose furious ravening fangs shall rend and tear thee;
Wrenching thy vitals forth, with the heart and midriff;
While inexpressible Tartesian monsters,
And grim Tithrasian Gorgons toss and scatter
With clattering claws, thine intertwined intestines.
To them, with instant summons, I repair,
Moving in hasty march with steps of speed.

  [*Æacus departs with a tremendous tragical exit,
   and Bacchus falls to the ground in a fright.*

Xan. Holloh, you! What's the matter there—?

Bac.   Oh dear,
I've had an accident.

Xan.   Poh! poh! jump up!
  Come! you ridiculous simpleton! don't lie there,
  The people will see you.
Bac.   Indeed I'm sick at heart; lah!
                (*Here a few lines are omitted.*)
Xan. Was there ever in heaven or earth such a coward?
Bac.   **Me?**
   A coward! Did not I show my presence of mind—
   And call for a sponge and water in a moment?
   Would a coward have done that?
Xan.   What else would he do?
Bac. He'd have lain there stinking like a nasty coward;
   But I jump'd up at once, like a lusty wrestler,
   And look'd about, and wiped myself, withal.
Xan. Most manfully done!
Bac.   By Jove, and I think it was;
   But tell me, wer'n't you frighten'd with that speech?
   —Such horrible expressions!
Xan. (*coolly, but with conscious and intentional coolness*).
                    No, not I;
   I took no notice—
Bac.   Weil, I'll tell you what,
   Since you're such a valiant-spirited kind of fellow,
   Do you be *Me*—with the club and the lion-skin,
   Now you're in this courageous temper of mind;
   And I'll go take my turn and carry the bundles.
Xan. Well—give us hold—I must humour you, forsooth;
   Make haste (*he changes his dress*), and now behold the
      Xanthian Hercules,
   And mind if I don't display more heart and spirit.
Bac. Indeed, and you look the character, completely,
   Like that heroic Melitensian hangdog—
   Come, now for my bundles. I must mind my bundles.

Enter Proserpine's Servant Maid (*a kind of Dame Quickly*), *who immediately addresses* Xanthias.

Dear Hercules. Well, you're come at last. Come in,
For the goddess, as soon as she heard of it, set to work
Baking peck loaves and frying stacks of pancakes,
And making messes of furmety; there's an ox
Besides, she has roasted whole, with a relishing stuffing,
If you'll only just step in this way.

Xan. (*with dignity and reserve*). I thank you,
I'm equally obliged.

Ser. Maid.   No, no, by Jupiter!
We must not let you off, indeed. There's wild fowl
And sweetmeats for the dessert, and the best of wine;
Only walk in.

Xan. (*as before*). I thank you. You'll excuse me.

Ser. Maid. No, no, we can't excuse you, indeed we can't;
There are dancing and singing girls besides.

Xan. (*with dissembled emotion*).   What! dancers?

Ser. Maid. Yes, that there are; the sweetest, charmingest
    things
That you ever saw—and there's the cook this moment
Is dishing up the dinner.

Xan. (*with an air of lofty condescension*). Go before then,
And tell the girls—those singing girls you mentioned—
To prepare for my approach in person presently.
    (*To Bacchus.*) You, sirrah! follow behind me with the
    bundles.

Bac. Holloh, you! what, do you take the thing in earnest,
Because, for a joke, I drest you up like Hercules?
            [*Xanthias continues to gesticulate as Hercules.*
Come, don't stand fooling, Xanthias. You'll provoke me.
There, carry the bundles, Sirrah, when I bid you.

Xan. (relapsing at once into his natural air).

    Why, sure? do you mean to take the things away

    That you gave me yourself of your own accord this in-
       stant?

Bac. I never mean a thing; I do it at once.

    Let go of the lion's skin directly, I tell you.

*Xan. (resigning his heroical insignia with a tragical air
    and tone).*

    To you, just Gods, I make my last appeal,

    Bear witness!

Bac.   What! the Gods?—do you think they mind you?

    How could you take it in your head, I wonder;

    Such a foolish fancy for a fellow like you,

    A mortal and a slave, to pass for Hercules?

Xan. There. Take them.—There—you may have them—
    but, please God,

    You may come to want my help some time or other.

CHORUS.

    Dexterous and wily wits,

        Find their own advantage ever;

    For the wind where'er it sits,

        Leaves a berth secure and clever

    To the ready navigator;

    That foresees and knows the nature,

    Of the wind can turn and shift

    To the sheltered easy side;

    'Tis a practice proved and tried,

    Not to wear a formal face; ⎫

    Fixt in attitude and place, ⎬

    Like an image on its base; ⎭

    'Tis the custom of the seas, ⎫

    Which, as all the world agrees, ⎬

    Justifies Theramenes. ⎭

BACCHUS.

How ridiculous and strange;
  What a monstrous proposition,
That I should condescend to change
  My dress, my name, and my condition,
To follow Xanthias, and behave
Like a mortal and a slave;
To be set to watch the door
While he wallow'd with his whore,
Tumbling on a purple bed;
  While I waited with submission,
To receive a broken head;
  Or be kick'd upon suspicion
Of impertinence and peeping
At the joys that he was reaping.

Enter Two WOMEN, *Sutlers or Keepers of an Eating House.*

1st *Woman.* What, Platana! Goody Platana! there! that'.
  he,
  The fellow that robs and cheats poor victuallers;
  That came to our house and eat those nineteen loaves.
2nd *Woman.* Ay, sure enough that's he, the very man.
Xan. (*tauntingly to Bacchus*). There's mischief in the
  wind for somebody!
1st *Woman.*—And a dozen and a half of cutlets and fried
  chops,
  At a penny halfpenny a piece—
Xan. (*significantly*).   There are pains and penalties
  Impending—
1st *Woman.*—And all the garlic: such a quantity
  As he swallowed—
Bac. (*delivers this speech with Herculean dignity, after his*

*fashion; having hitherto remained silent upon the same
principle*).

            Woman, you're beside yourself;
You talk you know not what—

2nd Woman.   No, no! you reckoned
I should not know you again with them there buskins.

1st Woman.—Good lack! and there was all that fish besides.
Indeed—with the pickle, and all—and the good green cheese
That he gorged at once, with the rind, and the rush-baskets;
And then, when I called for payment, he looked fierce,
And stared at me in the face, and grinned, and roared—

Xan. Just like him! That's the way wherever he goes.

1st Woman.—And snatched his sword out, and behaved like mad.

Xan. Poor souls! you suffered sadly!

1st Woman.   Yes, indeed;
And then we both ran off with the fright and terror,
And scrambled into the loft beneath the roof;
And he took up two rugs and stole them off.

Xan. Just like him again—but something must be done.
Go call me Cleon, he's my advocate.

2nd Woman. And Hyperbolus, if you meet him send him here.
He's mine; and we'll demolish him, I warrant.

1st Woman (*going close up to Bacchus in the true terma-
gant attitude of rage and defiance, with the arms
akimbo, and a neck and chin thrust out*).
How I should like to strike those ugly teeth out
With a good big stone, you ravenous greedy villain!
You gormandising villain! that I should—
Yes, that I should; your wicked ugly fangs

That have eaten up my substance, and devoured me.
Bac. And I could toss you into the public pit
  With the malefactors' carcasses; that I could,
  With pleasure and satisfaction; that I could.
1st Woman. And I should like to rip that gullet out
  With a reaping hook that swallowed all my tripe,
  And liver and lights—but I'll fetch Cleon here,
  And he shall summon him. He shall settle him,
  And have it out of him this very day.

                [Exeunt 1st and 2nd Woman.

Bac. (in a pretended soliloquy).
  I love poor Xanthias dearly, that I do;
  I wish I might be hanged else.
Xan.   Yes, I know—
  I know your meaning—No; no more of that,
  I won't act Hercules—
Bac.   Now pray don't say so,
  My little Xanthias.
Xan.   How should I be Hercules?
  A mortal and a slave, a fellow like me?—
Bac. I know you're angry, and you've a right to be angry;
  And if you beat me for it I'd not complain;
  But if ever I strip you again, from this time forward,
  I wish I may be utterly confounded,
  With my wife, my children, and my family,
  And the blear-eyed Archedemus into the bargain.
Xan. I agree then, on that oath, and those conditions.

    [Xanthias equips himself with the club and lion's
    skin, and Bacchus resumes his bundles.

    CHORUS *(addressing* XANTHIAS*).*

    Now that you revive and flourish
      In your old attire again,

You must rouse afresh and nourish
  Thoughts of an heroic strain;
That exalt and raise the figure,
And assume a fire and vigour;
And an attitude and air
Suited to the garb you wear;
With a brow severely bent,
Like the god you represent.
      But beware,
      Have a care!
If you blunder, or betray
Any weakness any way;
Weakness of the heart or brain,
We shall see you once again
Trudging in the former track,
With the bundles at your back.

XANTHIAS (*in reply to the* CHORUS).

Friends, I thank you for your care;
Your advice was good and fair;
Corresponding in its tone
With reflections of my own.
—Though I clearly comprehend
All the upshot and the end
(That if any good comes of it,
Any pleasure any profit—
He, my master, will recede
From the terms that were agreed),
You shall see me, notwithstanding,
Stern, intrepid, and commanding.
Now's the time; For there's a noise!
Now for figure, look, and voice!

Æacus *enters again as a vulgar executioner of the law, with
suitable understrappers in attendance.*

Æacus. Arrest me there that fellow that stole the dog.
There!—Pinion him!—Quick!

Bac. (*tauntingly to Xanthias*). There's somebody in a
scrape.

Xan. (*in a menacing attitude*). Keep off, and be hanged.

Æacus.   Oh, hoh! do you mean to fight for it?
Here! Pardokas, and Skeblias, and the rest of ye,
Make up to the rogue, and settle him. Come, be quick.
    [*A scuffle ensues, in which Xanthias succeeds in
        obliging Æacus's runners to keep their distance.*

Bac. (*mortified at Xanthias's prowess*).
Well, is not this quite monstrous and outrageous,
To steal the dog, and then to make an assault
In justification of it.

Xan. (*triumphantly and ironically*). Quite outrageous!

Æacus (*gravely, and dissembling his mortification*).
An aggravated case!

Xan. (*with candour and gallantry*). Well, now—by Jupiter,
May I die; but I never saw this place before—
Nor ever stole the amount of a farthing from you:
Nor a hair of your dog's tail—But you shall see now,
I'll settle all this business nobly and fairly.
—This slave of mine—you may take and torture him;
And if you make out anything against me,
You may take and put me to death for aught I care.

Æacus (*in an obliging tone, softened into deference and
civility by the liberality of Xanthias's proposal*).
But which way would you please to have him tortured?

Xan. (*with a gentlemanly spirit of accommodation*).
In your own way—with . . . the lash—with . . . knots
and screws,

With . . . the common usual customary tortures.

With the rack—with . . . the water-torture—anyway—

With fire and vinegar—all sorts of ways.

(*After a very slight pause.*)   There's only one thing I
  should warn you of:

I must not have him treated like a child,

To be whipt with fennel, or with lettuce leaves.

Æacus.   That's fair—and if so be . . . he's maim'd or
  crippled

In any respect—the valy shall be paid you.

Xan.   Oh no!—by no means! not to me!—by no means!

You must not mention it!—Take him to the torture.

Æacus.   It had better be here, and under your own eye.

(*To Bacchus.*)   Come you—put down your bundles and
  make ready.

And mind—Let me hear no lies

Bac.   I'll tell you what:

I'd advise people not to torture me;

I give you notice—I'm a deity.

So mind now—you'll have nobody to blame

But your own self—

Æacus.   What's that you're saying there?

Bac.   Why that I'm Bacchus, Jupiter's own son:

That fellow there's a slave.   [*Pointing to Xanthias.*

Æacus (*to Xanthias*).   Do ye hear?

Xan.   I hear him—

A reason the more to give him a good beating;

If he's immortal he need never mind it.

Bac.   Why should not you be beat as well as I then,

If you're immortal, as you say you are?

Xan.   Agreed—and him, the first that you see flinching,

Or seeming to mind it at all, you may set him down

For an impostor and no real deity.

Æacus (*to Xanthias with warmth and cordiality*).

  Ah, you're a worthy gentleman I'll be bound for't;

  You're all for the truth and the proof. Come—Strip there
both o' ye.

Xan. But how can ye put us to the question fairly,

  Upon equal terms?

Æacus (*in the tone of a person proposing a convenient,
agreeable arrangement*). Oh, easily enough,

  Conveniently enough—a lash a piece,

  Each in your turn; you can have 'em one by one.

Xan. That's right. (*Putting himself in an attitude to receive the blow.*) Now mind if ye see me flinch or
swerve.

Æacus (*striking Xanthias*). I've struck you.

Xan. No by Zeus! I never felt it.

Æacus. Well then I'll beat this other fellow. (*Striking
Bacchus.*)

Bac. When?

Æacus. I've struck already.

Bac. And I didn't even sneeze?

Æacus. No answer there. I'll try the other again. (*Striking Xanthias.*)

Xan. Won't you ever stop? Oh, woe!

Æacus. What! Woe?

  Were you hurt then?

Xan. No, by Zeus, I was only thinking

  Of my feast of Hercules in Diomea.

Æacus. Holy man. I must go back to the other one again.

Bac. Ho! Ho!

Æacus. What's that?

Bac. I saw some horsemen.

Æacus. But what are you weeping for?

Bac. I'm smelling onions.

Æacus. And you don't mind the blows at all?

Bac. Oh, not at all.

Æacus. Well, here we go, back to the other one.

Xan. Oh, ouch!

Æacus. What's that?

Xan. (*lifting his foot*). Pull out this thorn.

Æacus. What a job this is! I'll try the other again.

Bac. Apollo! (*a cry which he continues as if it were a quotation*) thou of Delos and of Pytho.

Xan. He's hurt. Didn't you hear him?

Bac. Me? Not I!

I just remembered a verse from Hipponax.

Xan. (*to Æacus*). You're getting nowhere. Beat him on the flanks.

Æacus. No, by Zeus, here's better. Turn up your belly.

Bac. Poseidon!

Xan. There, he's flinching. Did you hear him?

Bac. (*continuing the quotation from Sophocles*).

Who rulest the Ægean peaks and streams
And over the depths of the sea.

Æacus. Well, after all my pains, I'm quite at a loss
To discover which is the true, real deity.
By the Holy Goddess—I'm completely puzzled;
I must take you before Proserpine and Pluto,
Being gods themselves they're likeliest to know.

Bac. Why, that's a lucky thought. I only wish
It had happen'd to occur before you beat us.

CHORUS.

Muse, attend our solemn summons
And survey the assembled commons,
Congregated as they sit,
An enormous mass of wit,

—Full of genius, taste, and fire,
Jealous pride, and critic ire—
Cleophon among the rest
(Like the swallow from her nest,
A familiar foreign bird),
Chatters loud and will be heard,
(With the accent and the grace
Which he brought with him from Thrace);
But we fear the tuneful strain
Will be turn'd to grief and pain;
He must sing a dirge perforce
When his trial takes its course;
We shall hear him moan and wail,
Like the plaintive nightingale.

EPIRREMA.

It behoves the sacred Chorus, and of right to them belongs,
To suggest the best advice in their addresses and their songs,
In performance of our office, we present with all humility
A proposal for removing groundless fears and disability.
First that all that were inveigled into Phrynichus's treason,
Should be suffer'd and received by rules of evidence and reason
To clear their conduct—Secondly, that none of our Athenian race
Should live suspected and subjected to loss of franchise and disgrace,
Feeling it a grievous scandal when a single naval fight
Renders foreigners and slaves partakers of the city's right:

—Not that we condemn the measure; we conceived it
wisely done,

As a just and timely measure, and the first and only one:

—But your kinsmen and your comrades, those with
whom you fought and bore

Danger, hardship, and fatigue, or with their fathers long
before,

Struggling on the land and ocean, labouring with the
spear and oar

—These we think, as they profess repentance for their
past behaviour,

Might, by your exalted wisdom, be received to grace
and favour.

Better it would be, believe us, casting off revenge and
pride,

To receive as friends and kinsmen all that combat on
our side

Into full and equal franchise: on the other hand we fear,

If your hearts are fill'd with fancies, haughty, captious,
and severe;

While the shock of instant danger threatens shipwreck
to the state,

Such resolves will be lamented and repented of too late.

> If the Muse forsees at all ⎫
> What in future will befall ⎬
> Dirty Cleigenes the small— ⎭
> He, the sovereign of the bath,
> Will not long escape from scath;
> But must perish by and by, ⎫
> With his potash and his lye; ⎬
> With his realm and dynasty, ⎭

His terraqueous scouring ball,
And his washes, one and all;
Therefore he can never cease
To declaim against a peace.

ANTEPIRREMA.

Often times have we reflected on a similar abuse,
In the choice of men for office, and of coins for common
use;
For your old and standard pieces, valued, and approved,
and tried,
Here among the Grecian nations, and in all the world
beside;
Recognised in every realm for trusty stamp and pure
assay,
Are rejected and abandon'd for the trash of yesterday;
For a vile, adulterate issue, drossy, counterfeit, and base,
Which the traffic of the city passes current in their place!
And the men that stood for office, noted for acknowl-
edged worth,
And for manly deeds of honour, and for honourable
birth;
Train'd in exercise and art, in sacred dances and in song,
All are ousted and supplanted by a base ignoble throng;
Paltry stamp and vulgar mettle raise them to command
and place,
Brazen counterfeit pretenders, scoundrels of a scoundrel
race;
Whom the state in former ages scarce would have allow'd
to stand,
At the sacrifice of outcasts, as the scape-goats of the land.
—Time it is—and long has been, renouncing all your
follies past,

To recur to sterling merit and intrinsic worth at last.

—If we rise, we rise with honour; if we fall, it must be so!

—But there was an ancient saying, which we all have heard and know,

That the wise, in dangerous cases, have esteem'd it safe and good

To receive a slight chastisement from *a wand of noble wood*.

Scene. XANTHIAS *and* ÆACUS.

Æacus. By Jupiter; but he's a gentleman,
  That master of yours.

Xan.   A gentleman! To be sure he is;
  Why, he does nothing else but wench and drink.

Æacus. His never striking you when you took his name—
  Outfacing him and contradicting him!—

Xan. It might have been worse for him if he had.

Æacus. Well, that's well spoken, like a true-bred slave.
  It's just the sort of language I delight in.

Xan. You love excuses?

Æacus.   Yes; but I prefer
  Cursing my master quietly in private.

Xan. Mischief you're fond of?

Æacus.   Very fond indeed.

Xan. What think ye of muttering as you leave the room
  After a beating?

Æacus.   Why, that's pleasant too.

Xan. By Jove, is it! But listening at the door
  To hear their secrets?

Æacus.   Oh, there's nothing like it.

Xan. And then the reporting them in the neighbourhood.

Æacus. That's beyond everything.—That's quite ecstatic.
Xan. Well, give me your hand. And, there, take mine—
    and buss me.
  And there again—and now for Jupiter's sake!—
  (For he's the patron of our cuffs and beatings)
  Do tell me what's that noise of people quarrelling
  And abusing one another there within?
Æacus. Æschylus and Euripides, only!
Xan.   Heh?—?—?
Æacus. Why, there's a desperate business has broke out
  Among these here dead people;—quite a tumult.
Xan. As how?
Æacus.   First, there's a custom we have establish'd
  In favour of professors of the arts.
  When any one, the first in his own line,
  Comes down amongst us here, he stands entitled
  To privilege and precedence, with a seat
  At Pluto's royal board.
Xan.   I understand you.
Æacus. So he maintains it, till there comes a better
  Of the same sort, and then resigns it up.
Xan. But why should Æschylus be disturb'd at this?
Æacus. He held the seat for tragedy, as the master
  In that profession.
Xan.   Well, and who's there now?
Æacus. He kept it till Euripides appeared;
  But he collected audiences about him,
  And flourish'd, and exhibited, and harangued
  Before the thieves, and housebreakers, and rogues,
  Cut-purses, cheats, and vagabonds, and villains,
  That make the mass of population here;
                 [Pointing to the audience.

And they—being quite transported, and delighted
With his equivocations and evasions,
His subtleties and niceties and quibbles—
In short—they raised an uproar, and declared him
Archpoet, by a general acclamation.
And he with this grew proud and confident,
And laid a claim to the seat where Æschylus sat.

Xan. And did not he get pelted for his pains?

Æacus (*with the dry concise importance of superior local information*).

Why, no—The mob call'd out, and it was carried,
To have a public trial of skill between them.

Xan. You mean the mob of scoundrels that you mention'd?

Æacus. Scoundrels indeed! Ay, scoundrels without number.

Xan. But Æschylus must have had good friends and hearty?

Æacus. Yes; but good men are scarce both here and elsewhere.

Xan. Well, what has Pluto settled to be done?

Æacus. To have an examination and a trial
In public.

Xan.   But how comes it?—Sophocles?—
Why does he not put forth his claim amongst them?

Æacus. No, no!—He's not the kind of man—not he!
I tell ye; the first moment that he came,
He went up to Æschylus and saluted him
And kiss'd his cheek and took his hand quite kindly;
And Æschylus edged a little from his seat
To give him room; so now the story goes,
(At least I had it from Cleidemides;)

He means to attend there as a stander-by,
Proposing to take up the conqueror;
If Æschylus gets the better, well and good,
He gives up his pretensions—but if not,
He'll stand a trial, he says, against Euripides.

Xan. There'll be strange doings.

Æacus.   That there will—and shortly
—Here—in this place—strange things, I promise you;
A kind of thing that no man could have thought of;
Why, you'll see poetry weigh'd out and measured.

Xan. What, will they bring their tragedies to the steel-
yards?

Æacus. Yes, will they—with their rules and compasses
They'll measure, and examine, and compare,
And bring their plummets, and their lines and levels,
To take the bearings—for Euripides
Says that he'll make a survey, word by word.

Xan. Æschylus takes the thing to heart, I doubt.

Æacus. He bent his brows and pored upon the ground; I
saw him.

Xan.   Well, but who decides the business?

Æacus. Why, there the difficulty lies—for judges,
True learned judges, are grown scarce, and Æschylus
Objected to the Athenians absolutely.

Xan. Considering them as rogues and villains mostly.

Æacus. As being ignorant and empty generally;
And in their judgment of the stage particularly.
In fine, they've fix'd upon that master of yours,
As having had some practice in the business.
But we must wait within—for when our masters
Are warm and eager, stripes and blows ensue.

CHORUS.

The full-mouth'd master of the tragic quire,
We shall behold him foam with rage and ire;
—Confronting in the list
His eager, shrewd, sharp-tooth'd antagonist.
Then will his visual orbs be wildly whirl'd
And huge invectives will be hurl'd
  Superb and supercilious,
  Atrocious, atrabilious,
With furious gesture and with lips of foam,
And lion crest unconscious of the comb;
Erect with rage—his brow's impending gloom
O'ershadowing his dark eyes' terrific blaze.
  The opponent, dexterous and wary,
  Will fend and parry:
While masses of conglomerated phrase,
  Enormous, ponderous, and pedantic,
  With indignation frantic,
  And strength and force gigantic,
    Are desperately sped
    At his devoted head—
Then in different style
The touchstone and the file,
And subleties of art
In turn will play their part;
Analysis and rule,
And every modern tool;
With critic scratch and scribble,
And nice invidious nibble;
Contending for the important choice,
A vast expenditure of human voice!

Scene. EURIPIDES, BACCHUS, ÆSCHYLUS.

Eur. Don't give me your advice, I claim the seat
  As being a better and superior artist.
Bac. What, Æschylus, don't you speak? you hear his lan
  guage.
Eur. He's mustering up a grand commanding visage
  —A silent attitude—the common trick
  That he begins with in his tragedies.
Bac. Come, have a care, my friend—You'll say too much.
Eur. I know the man of old—I've scrutinised
  And shown him long ago for what he is,
  A rude unbridled tongue, a haughty spirit;
  Proud, arrogant, and insolently pompous;
  Rough, clownish, boisterous, and overbearing.
Æs. Say'st thou me so? Thou bastard of the earth,
  With thy patch'd robes and rags of sentiment
  Raked from the streets and stitch'd and tack'd together/
  Thou mumping, whining, beggarly hypocrite!
  But you shall pay for it.
Bac. (*in addressing Æschylus attempts to speak in more ele
  vated style*). There now, Æschylus,
  You grow too warm. Restrain your ireful mood.
Æs. Yes; but I'll seize that sturdy beggar first,
  And search and strip him bare of his pretensions.
Bac. Quick! Quick! A sacrifice to the winds—Make
  ready;
  The storm of rage is gathering. Bring a victim.
Æs. —A wretch that has corrupted everything;
  Our music with his melodies from Crete;
  Our morals with incestuous tragedies.
Bac. Dear, worthy Æschylus, contain yourself,
  And as for you, Euripides, move off
  This instant, if you're wise; I give you warning.

Or else, with one of his big thumping phrases,
You'll get your brains dash'd out, and all your **notions**
And sentiments and matter mash'd to pieces.
—And thee, most noble Æschylus (*as above*), I beseech
With mild demeanour calm and affable
To hear and answer.—For it ill beseems
Illustrious bards to scold like market-women.
But you roar out and bellow like a furnace.

*Eur. (in the tone of a town blackguard working himself up
    for a quarrel).*

I'm up to it.—I'm resolved, and here I stand
Ready and steady—take what course you will;
Let him be first to speak, or else let me.
I'll match my plots and characters against him;
My sentiments and language, and what not:
Ay! and my music too, my Meleager,
My Æolus and my Telephus and all.

Bac. Well, Æschylus,—determine. What say you?

Æs. (speaks in a tone of grave manly despondency).

I wish the place of trial had been elsewhere,
I stand at disadvantage here.

Bac.   As how?

Æs. Because my poems live on earth above,
And his died with him, and descended here,
And are at hand as ready witnesses;
But you decide the matter: I submit.

Bac. (with official pertness and importance).

Come—let them bring me fire and frankincense,
That I may offer vows and make oblations
For any ingenious critical conclusion
To this same elegant and clever trial—

(To the Chorus.)

And you too,—sing me a hymn there.—To the Muses.

Chorus.

To the Heavenly Nine we petition,
Ye, that on earth or in air are for ever kindly protecting
the vagaries of learned ambition,
And at your ease from above our sense and folly direct-
ing (or poetical contests inspecting, ·
Deign to behold for a while as a scene of amusing attention, all the struggles of style and invention),
Aid, and assist, and attend, and afford to the furious
authors your refined and enlighten'd suggestions;
Grant them ability—force and agility, quick recollections,
and address in their answers and questions,
Pithy replies, with a word to the wise, and pulling and
hauling, with inordinate uproar and bawling,
Driving and drawing, like carpenters sawing, their
dramas asunder:
    With suspended sense and wonder,
    All are waiting and attending
    On the conflict now depending!

Bac. Come, say your prayers, you two before the trial.
                     [Æschylus offers incense.
Æs. O Ceres, nourisher of my soul, maintain me
  A worthy follower of thy mysteries.
Bac. (*to Euripides*). There, you there, make your offering.
Eur.   Well, I will;
  But I direct myself to other deities.
Bac. Hey, what? Your own? some new ones?
Eur.   Most assuredly!
Bac. Well! Pray away, then—to your own new deities.
                     [Euripides offers incense.
Eur. Thou foodful Air, the nurse of all notions;
  And ye, the organic powers of sense and speech,

And keen refined olfactory discernment,
Assist my present search for faults and errors.

Chorus.

Here beside you, here are we,
Eager all to hear and see
This abstruse and mighty battle
Of profound and learned prattle.
—But, as it appears to me,
Thus the course of it will be;
He, the junior and appellant,
Will advance as the assailant.
Aiming shrewd satyric darts
At his rival's noble parts;
And with sallies sharp and keen
Try to wound him in the spleen,
While the veteran rends and raises
Rifted, rough, uprooted phrases,
Wielded like a threshing staff
Scattering the dust and chaff.

Bac. Come, now begin, dispute away, but first I give you
     notice
   That every phrase in your discourse must be refined,
     avoiding
   Vulgar absurd comparisons, and awkward silly joking.
Eur. At the first outset, I forbear to state my own pre-
     tensions;
   Hereafter I shall mention them, when his have been
     refuted;
   After I shall have fairly shown, how he befool'd and
     cheated

The rustic audience that he found, which Phrynichus
  bequeathed him.
He planted first upon the stage a figure veil'd and
  muffled,
An Achilles or a Niobe, that never show'd their faces;
But kept a tragic attitude, without a word to utter.
Bac. No more they did: 'tis very true.
Eur.   —In the meanwhile the Chorus
  Strung on ten strophes right-an-end, but they remain'd in
  silence.
Bac. I liked that silence well enough, as well, perhaps, or
  better
Than those new talking characters—
Eur.   That's from your want of judgment,
  Believe me.
Bac.   Why, perhaps it is; but what was his intention?
Eur. Why, mere conceit and insolence; to keep the people
  waiting
Till Niobe should deign to speak, to drive his drama
  forward.
Bac. O what a rascal. Now I see the tricks he used to
  play me.
    [*To Æschylus, who is showing signs of indignation
      by various contortions.*
—What makes you writhe and winch about?—
Eur.   Because he feels my censures.
—Then having dragg'd and drawl'd along, half-way to
  the conclusion,
He foisted in a dozen words of noisy boisterous accent,
With lofty plumes and shaggy brows, mere bugbears of
  the language.
That no man ever heard before.—
Æs.   Alas! alas!

Bac. (*to Æschylus*).   Have done there!

Eur. He never used a simple word.

Bac. (*to Æschylus*). Don't grind your teeth so strangely.

Eur. But "Bulwarks and Scamanders" and "Hippogrifs
and Gorgons."

"On burnish'd shields emboss'd in brass;" bloody remorse-
less phrases

Which nobody could understand.

Bac.   Well, I confess, for my part,

I used to keep awake at night, with guesses and conjec-
tures

To think what kind of foreign bird he meant by griffin-
horses.

Æs. A figure on the heads of ships; you goose, you must
have seen them.

Bac. Well, from the likeness, I declare, I took it for Eruxis.

Eur. So! Figures from the heads of ships art fit for tragic
diction.

Æs. Well then—thou paltry wretch, explain. What were
your own devices?

Eur. Not stories about flying-stags, like yours, and griffin-
horses;

Nor terms nor images derived from tapestry Persian
hangings.

When I received the Muse from you I found her puff'd
and pamper'd

With pompous sentences and terms, a cumbrous huge
virago.

My first attention was applied to make her look genteelly;

And bring her to a slighter shape by dint of lighter diet:

I fed her with plain household phrase, and cool familiar
salad,

With water-gruel episode, with sentimental jelly,

With moral mincemeat; till at length I brought her into
    compass;
Cephisophon, who was my cook, contrived to make them
    relish.
I kept my plots distinct and clear, and, to prevent con-
    fusion,
My leading characters rehearsed their pedigrees for pro-
    logues.

Æs. 'Twas well, at least, that you forbore to quote your
    own extraction.

Eur. From the first opening of the scene, all persons were
    in action;
The master spoke, the slave replied, the women, young
    and old ones,
All had their equal share of talk—

Æs.   Come, then, stand forth and tell us,
What forfeit less than death is due for such an in-
    novation?

Eur. I did it upon principle, from democratic motives.

Bac. Take care, my friend—upon that ground your foot-
    ing is but ticklish.

Eur. I taught these youths to speechify.

Æs.   I say so too.—Moreover
I say that—for the public good—you ought to have been
    hang'd first.

Eur. The rules and forms of rhetoric,—the laws of compo-
    sition,
To prate—to state—and in debate to meet a question
    fairly:
At a dead lift to turn and shift—to make a nice distinc-
    tion.

Æs. I grant it all—I make it all—my ground of accusation.

Eur. The whole in cases and concerns occurring and re-
  curring
  At every turn and every day domestic and familiar,
  So that the audience, one and all, from personal experi-
  ence,
  Were competent to judge the piece, and form a fair
  opinion
  Whether my scenes and sentiments agreed with truth
  and nature.
  I never took them by surprise to storm their understand-
  ings,
  With Memnons and Tydides's and idle rattle-trappings
  Of battle-steeds and clattering shields to scare them from
  their senses;
  But for a test (perhaps the best) our pupils and adherents
  May be distingush'd instantly by person and behaviour;
  His are Phormisius the rough, Meganetes the gloomy,
  Hobgoblin-headed, trumpet-mouth'd, grim-visaged, ugly-
  bearded;
  But mine are Cleitophon the smooth,—Theramenes the
  gentle.
Bac. Theramenes—a clever hand, a universal genius,
  I never found him at a loss in all the turns of party
  To change his watchword at a word or at a moment's
  warning.
Eur. Thus it was that I began,
  With a nicer, neater plan;
  Teaching men to look about,
  Both within doors and without;
  To direct their own affairs,
  And their house and household wares;
  Marking everything amiss—
  "Where is that? and—What is this?"

"This is broken—that is gone."
'Tis the modern style and tone.
Bac. Yes, by Jove—and at their homes
Nowadays each master comes,
Of a sudden bolting in
With an uproar and a din;
Rating all the servants round,
"If it's lost, it must be found.
Why was all the garlic wasted?
There, that honey has been tasted:
And these olives pilfer'd here.
Where's the pot we bought last year?
What's become of all the fish?
Which of you has broke the dish?"
Thus it is, but heretofore,
The moment that they cross'd the door,
They sat them down to doze and snore.

CHORUS.

"Noble Achilles! you see the disaster,
    The shame and affront, and an enemy nigh!"
Oh! bethink thee, mighty master,
    Think betimes of your reply;
Yet beware, lest anger force
Your hasty chariot from the course;
Grievous charges have been heard,
With many a sharp and bitter word,
Notwithstanding, mighty chief,
Let Prudence fold her cautious reef
In your anger's swelling sail;
By degrees you may prevail,
But beware of your behaviour
Till the wind is in your favour:

Now for your answer, illustrious architect,
  Founder of lofty theatrical lays!
Patron in chief of our tragical trumperies!
  Open the floodgate of figure and phrase!

Æs. My spirit is kindled with anger and shame,
  To so base a competitor forced to reply,
  But I needs must retort, or the wretch will report
  That he left me refuted and foil'd in debate;
  Tell me then, What are the principal merits
  Entitling a poet to praise and renown?
Eur. The improvement of morals, the progress of mind,
  When a poet, by skill and invention,
  Can render his audience virtuous and wise.
Æs. But if you, by neglect or intention,
  Have done the reverse, and from brave honest spirits
  Depraved, and have left them degraded and base,
  Tell me, what punishment ought you to suffer?
Bac. Death, to be sure!—Take that answer from me.
Æs. Observe then, and mark, what our citizens were,
  When first from my care they were trusted to you;
  Not scoundrel informers, or paltry buffoons,
  Evading the services due to the state;
  But with hearts all on fire, for adventure and war,
  Distinguished for hardiness, stature, and strength,
  Breathing forth nothing but lances and darts,
  Arms, and equipment, and battle array,
  Bucklers, and shields, and habergeons, and hauberks,
  Helmets, and plumes, and heroic attire.
Bac. There he goes, hammering on with his helmets,
  He'll be the death of me one of these days.
Eur. But how did you manage to make 'em so manly,
  What was the method, the means that you took?

Bac. Speak, Æschylus, speak, and behave yourself better,
   And don't in your rage stand so silent and stern.
Æs. A drama, brimful with heroical spirit.
Eur. What did you call it?
Æs.   "The Chiefs against Thebes,"
   That inspired each spectator with martial ambition,
   Courage, and ardour, and prowess, and pride.
Bac. But you did very wrong to encourage the Thebans.
   Indeed, you deserve to be punish'd, you do,
   For the Thebans are grown to be capital soldiers,
   You've done us a mischief by that very thing.
Æs. The fault was your own, if you took other courses;
   The lesson I taught was directed to you:
   Then I gave you the glorious theme of "the Persians,"
   Replete with sublime patriotical strains,
   The record and example of noble achievement,
   The delight of the city, the pride of the stage.
Bac. I rejoiced, I confess, when the tidings were carried
   To old King Darius, so long dead and buried,
   And the chorus in concert kept wringing their hands,
   Weeping and wailing, and crying, Alas!
Æs. Such is the duty, the task of a poet,
   Fulfilling in honour his office and trust.
   Look to traditional history—look
   To antiquity, primitive, early, remote:
   See there, what a blessing illustrious poets
   Conferred on mankind, in the centuries past,
   Orpheus instructed mankind in religion,
   Reclaim'd them from bloodshed and barbarous rites:
   Musæus deliver'd the doctrine of medicine,
   And warnings prophetic for ages to come:
   Next came old Hesiod, teaching us husbandry,
   Ploughing, and sowing, and rural affairs,

Rural economy, rural astronomy,
Homely morality, labour, and thrift:
Homer himself, our adorable Homer,
What was his title to praise and renown?
What, but the worth of the lessons he taught us,
Discipline, arms, and equipment of war?

Bac. Yes, but Pantacles was never the wiser;
For in the procession he ought to have led,
When his helmet was tied, he kept puzzling, and tried
To fasten the crest on the crown of his head.

Æs. But other brave warriors and noble commanders
Were train'd in his lessons to valour and skill;
Such was the noble heroical Lamachus;
Others besides were instructed by him;
And I, from his fragments ordaining a banquet,
Furnish'd and deck'd with majestical phrase,
Brought forward the models of ancient achievement,
Teucer, Patroclus, and chiefs of antiquity;
Raising and rousing Athenian hearts,
When the signal of onset was blown in their ear,
With a similar ardour to dare and to do;
But I never allow'd of your lewd Sthenobœas,
Or filthy, detestable Phædras—not I—
Indeed, I should doubt if my drama throughout
Exhibit an instance of woman in love.

Eur. No, you were too stern for an amorous turn,
For Venus and Cupid too stern and too stupid.

Æs. May they leave me at rest, and with peace in my breast,
And infest and pursue your kindred and you,
With the very same blow that despatch'd you below.

Bac. That was well enough said; with the life that he led,
He himself in the end got a wound from a friend.

Eur. But what, after all, is the horrible mischief?

My poor Sthenobœas, what harm have they done?

Æs. The example is followed, the practice has gain'd,
And women of family, fortune, and worth,
Bewilder'd with shame in a passionate fury,
Have poison'd themselves for Bellerophon's sake.

Eur. But at least you'll allow that I never invented it,
Phædra's affair was a matter of fact.

Æs. A fact, with a vengeance! but horrible facts
Should be buried in silence, not bruited abroad,
Nor brought forth on the stage, nor emblazon'd in poetry,
Children and boys have a teacher assign'd them—
The bard is a master for manhood and youth,
Bound to instruct them in virtue and truth,
Beholden and bound.

Eur.   But is virtue a sound?
Can any mysterious virtue be found
In bombastical, huge, hyperbolical phrase?

Æs. Thou dirty, calamitous wretch, recollect
That exalted ideas of fancy require
To be clothed in a suitable vesture of phrase;
And that heroes and gods may be fairly supposed
Discoursing in words of a mightier import,
More lofty by far than the children of man;
As the pomp of apparel assign'd to their persons,
Produced on the stage and presented to view,
Surpasses in dignity, splendour, and lustre
Our popular garb and domestic attire,
A practice which nature and reason allow,
But which you disannull'd and rejected.

Eur.   As how?

Æs. When you brought forth your kings, in a villainous fashion,
In patches and rags, as a claim for compassion.

Eur. And this is a grave misdemeanour, forsooth!

Æs. It has taught an example of sordid untruth;
   For the rich of the city, that ought to equip,
   And to serve with, a ship, are appealing to pity,
   Pretending distress—with an overworn dress.

Bac. By Jove, so they do; with a waistcoat brand new,
   Worn closely within, warm and new for the skin;
   And if they escape in this beggarly shape,
   You'll meet 'em at market, I warrant 'em all,
   Buying the best at the fishmonger's stall.

Æs. He has taught every soul to sophisticate truth;
   And debauch'd all the bodies and minds of the youth;
   Leaving them morbid, and pallid, and spare;
   And the places of exercise vacant and bare:—
   The disorder has spread to the fleet and the crew;
   The service is ruin'd, and ruin'd by you—
   With prate and debate in a mutinous state;
   Whereas, in my day, 'twas a different way;
   Nothing they said, nor knew nothing to say,
   But to call for their porridge, and cry, "Pull away."

Bac. Yes—yes, they knew this,
   How to f . . . in the teeth
   Of the rower beneath;
   And befoul their own comrades,
   And pillage ashore;
   But now they forget the command of the oar:—
   Prating and splashing,
   Discussing and dashing,
   They steer here and there,
   With their eyes in the air,
   Hither and thither,
   Nobody knows whither.

Æs. Can the reprobate mark in the course he has run,
   One crime unattempted, a mischief undone?

With his horrible passions, of sisters and brothers,
And sons-in-laws, tempted by villainous mothers,
And temples defiled with a bastardly birth,
And women, divested of honour or worth,
That talk about life "as a death upon earth;"
And sophistical frauds and rhetorical bawds;
Till now the whole state is infested with tribes
Of scriveners and scribblers, and rascally scribes—
All practice of masculine vigour and pride,
Our wrestling and running, are all laid aside,
And we see that the city can hardly provide
For the Feast of the Founders, a racer of force
To carry the torch and accomplish a course.

Bac. Well, I laugh'd till I cried
  The last festival tide,
  At the fellow that ran,—
  'Twas a heavy fat man,
  And he panted and hobbled,
  And stumbled and wabbled,
  And the pottery people about the gate,
  Seeing him hurried, and tired, and late,
  Stood to receive him in open rank,
  Helping him on with a hearty spank
  Over the shoulder and over the flank,
  The flank, the loin, the back, the shoulders,
  With shouts of applause from all beholders;
  While he ran on with a filthy fright,
  Puffing his link to keep it alight.

CHORUS.

  Ere the prize is lost and won
  Mighty doings will be done.
  Now then—(though to judge aright
  Is difficult, when force and might

Are opposed with ready slight,
When the Champion that is cast
Tumbles uppermost at last)
—Since you meet in equal match,
Argue, contradict and scratch,
Scuffle, and abuse and bite
Tear and fight,
With all your wits and all your **might**.
—Fear not for a want of sense
Or judgment in your audience,
That defect has been removed;
They're prodigiously improved,
Disciplined, alert and smart,
Drill'd and exercised in art:
Each has got a little book,
In the which they read and look,
Doing all their best endeavour
To be critical and clever;
Thus their own ingenious natures,
  Aided and improved by learning,
Will provide you with spectators
  Shrewd, attentive, and discerning.

Terrestrial Hermes with supreme espial,
Inspector of that old paternal realm,
Aid and assist me now, you suppliant,
Revisiting and returning to my country!

Eur. It is not justly express'd, since he return'd
  Clandestinely without authority.
Bac. That's well remark'd; but I don't comprehend it.
Eur. (*tauntingly and coolly*).
  Proceed—Continue!

Bac. (*jealous of his authority*). Yes, you must continue,
  Æschylus, I command you to continue.
(*To Euripides.*)
  And you, keep a look-out and mark his blunders.
Æs. "From his sepulchral mound I call my father
  "To listen and hear"—
Eur.   There's a tautology!
  "To listen and hear—"
Bac.   Why, don't you see, you ruffian!
  It's a dead man he's calling to—Three times
  We call to 'em, but they can't be made to hear.
Æs. And you: your prologues, of what kind were they?
Eur. I'll show ye; and if you'll point out a tautology,
  Or a single word clapt in to botch a verse—
  That's all!—I'll give you leave to spit upon me.
Bac. (*with an absurd air of patience and resignation*).
  Well, I can't help myself; I'm bound to attend.
  Begin then with these same fine-spoken prologues.
Eur. "Œdipus was at first a happy man." . . .
Æs. Not he, by Jove!—but born to misery;
  Predicted and predestined by an oracle
  Before his birth to murder his own father!
  —Could he have been "at first a happy man?"
Eur. . . . "But afterwards became a wretched mortal."
Æs. By no means! he continued to be wretched,
  —Born wretched, and exposed as soon as born
  Upon a potsherd in a winter's night;
  Brought up a foundling with disabled feet;
  Then married—a young man to an aged woman,
  That proved to be his mother—whereupon
  He tore his eyes out.
Bac.   To complete his happiness,
  He ought to have served at sea with Erasinides.

There!—that's enough—now come to music, can't ye?
Eur.   I mean it; I shall now proceed to expose him
As a bad composer, awkward, uninventive,
Repeating the same strain perpetually.—

CHORUS.

I stand in wonder and perplext
To think of what will follow next.
Will he dare to criticise
The noble bard, that did devise
Our oldest, boldest harmonies,
Whose mighty music we revere?
Much I marvel, much I fear.—

Eur.   Mighty fine music, truly! I'll give ye a sample;
It's every inch cut out to the same pattern.
Bac.   I'll mark—I've pick'd these pebbles up for counters.
Eur.   Noble Achilles! Forth to the rescue!
Forth to the rescue with ready support!
Hasten and go,
There is havoc and woe,
Hasty defeat,
And a bloody retreat,
Confusion and rout,
And the terrible shout
Of a conquering foe,
Tribulation and woe!
Bac.   Whoh hoh there! we've had woes enough, I reckon;
Therefore I'll go to wash away my woe
In a warm bath.
Eur.   No, do pray wait an instant,
And let me give you first another strain,
Transferr'd to the stage from music to the lyre.

Bac. Proceed then—only give us no more woes.

Eur. The supremacy sceptre and haughty command
Of the Grecian land—with a flatto-flatto-flatto-thrat—
And the ravenous sphinx, with her horrible brood,
Thirsting for blood—with a flatto-flatto-flatto-thrat,
And armies equipt for a vengeful assault,
For Paris's fault—with a flatto-flatto-flatto-thrat.

Bac. What herb is that same flatto-thrat? some simple,
I guess, you met with in the field of Marathon:
—But such a tune as this! you must have learnt it
From fellows hauling buckets at the well.

Æs. Such were the strains I purified and brought
To just perfection—taught by Phrynichus,
Not copying him, but culling other flowers
From those fair meadows which the Muses love—
—But he filches and begs, adapts and borrows
Snatches of tunes from minstrels in the street,
Strumpets and vagabonds—the lullabys
Of nurses and old women—jigs and ballads—
I'll give ye a proof—Bring me a lyre here, somebody.
What signifies a lyre? the castanets
Will suit him better—Bring the castanets,
With Euripides's Muse to snap her fingers
In cadence to her master's compositions.

Bac. This Muse, I take it, is a Lesbian Muse.

Æs. Gentle halcyons, ye that lave
    Your snowy plume,
  Sporting on the summer wave;
    Ye too that around the room,
  On the rafters of the roofs
  Strain aloft your airy woof;
  Ye spiders, spiders ever spinning,
  Never ending, still beginning—

Where the dolphin loves to follow,
Weltering in the surge's hollow,
Dear to Neptune and Apollo;
By the seamen understood
Ominous of harm or good;
In capricious, eager sallies,
Chasing, racing round the galleys.
Well now. Do you see this?

Bac. I see it—[*After which Æschylus turns to his antagonist:*]

Such is your music. I shall now proceed
To give a specimen of your monodies—

O dreary shades of night!
What phantoms of affright
Have scared my troubled sense
With saucer eyes immense;
And huge horrific paws
With bloody claws!
Ye maidens haste, and bring
From the fair spring

A bucket of fresh water; whose clear stream
May purify me from this dreadful dream:

But oh! my dream is out!
Ye maidens search about!

O mighty powers of mercy, can it be;
That Glyke, Glyke, she

(My friend and civil neighbour heretofore),
Has robb'd my henroost of its feather'd store?

With the dawn I was beginning,
Spinning, spinning, spinning, spinning,
Unconscious of the meditated crime;
Meaning to sell my yarn at market-time.

Now tears alone are left me,
My neighbour hath bereft me,
Of all—of all—of all—all but a tear!
Since he, my faithful trusty chanticleer
  Is flown—is flown!—Is gone—is gone!
—But, O ye nymphs of sacred Ida, bring
Torches and bows, with arrows on the string;
      And search around
  All the suspected ground:
And thou, fair huntress of the sky;
Deign to attend, descending from on high—
—While Hecate, with her tremendous torch,
Even from the topmost garret to the porch
Explores the premises with search exact,
  To find the thief and ascertain the fact—

Bac. Come, no more songs!
Æs.   I've had enough of 'em;
  For my part, I shall bring him to the balance,
  As a true test of our poetic merit,
  To prove the weight of our respective verses.
Bac. Well then, so be it—if it must be so,
  That I'm to stand here like a cheesemonger
  Retailing poetry with a pair of scales.

> [*A huge pair of scales are here discovered on the
> stage.*

CHORUS.

Curious eager wits pursue
Strange devices quaint and new,
Like the scene you witness here,
Unaccountable and queer;
I myself, if merely told it,
If I did not here behold it,

Should have deem'd it utter folly,
Craziness and nonsense wholly.

Bac.   Move up; stand close to the balance!
Eur.   Here are we—
Bac.   Take hold now, and each of you repeat a verse,
   And don't leave go before I call to you!
Eur.   We're ready.
Bac.   Now, then, each repeat a verse,
Eur.   "I wish that Argo with her woven wings."
Æs.   "O streams of Sperchius, and ye pastured plains."
Bac.   Let go!—See now—this scale outweighs that other.
   Very considerably—
Eur.   How did it happen?
Bac.   He slipp'd a river in, like the wool-jobbers,
   To moisten his metre—but your line was light,
   A thing with wings—ready to fly away.
Eur.   Let him try once again then, and take hold.
Bac.   Take hold once more.
Eur.   We're ready.
Bac.   Now repeat.
Eur.   "Speech is the temple and altar of persuasion."
Æs.   "Death is a God that loves no sacrifice."
Bac.   Let go!—See there again! This scale sinks down;
   No wonder that it should, with Death put into it,
   The heaviest of all calamities.
Eur.   But I put in persuasion finely express'd
   In the best terms.
Bac.   Perhaps so; but persuasion
   Is soft and light and silly—Think of something
   That's heavy and huge, to outweigh him, something solid.
Eur.   Let's see—Where have I got it? Something solid?
Bac.   "Achilles has thrown twice—Twice a deuce ace!"

Come now, one trial more; this is the last.

Eur. "He grasp'd a mighty mace of massy weight."

Æs. "Cars upon cars, and corpses heap'd pell mell."

Bac. He has nick'd you again—

Eur.   Why so? What has he done?

Bac. He had heap'd ye up cars and corpses, such a load
   As twenty Egyptian labourers could not carry—

Æs. Come, no more single lines—let him bring all,
   His wife, his children, his Cephisophon,
   His books and everything, himself to boot—
   I'll counterpoise them with a couple of lines.

Bac. Well, they're both friends of mine—I shan't decide
   To get myself ill-will from either party;
   One of them seems extraordinary clever,
   And the other suits my taste particularly.

Pluto. Won't you decide then, and conclude the business?

Bac. Suppose then I decide; what then?

Pluto.   Then take him
   Away with you, whichever you prefer,
   As a present for your pains in coming down here.

Bac. Heaven bless ye—Well—let's see now—Can't ye
      advise me?
   This is the case—I'm come in search of a poet—

Pluto. With what design?

Bac.   With this design; to see
   The City again restored to peace and wealth,
   Exhibiting tragedies in a proper style.
   —Therefore whichever gives the best advice
   On public matters I shall take him with me.
   —First then of Alcibiades, what think ye?
   The City is in hard labour with the question.

Eur. What are her sentiments towards him?

Bac.   What?

"She loves and she detests and longs to have him."
But tell me, both of you, your own opinions.

Eur. (*Euripides and Æschylus speak each in his own
tragical style*). I hate the man, that in his country's
service
Is slow, but ready and quick to work her harm;
Unserviceable except to serve himself.

Bac. Well said, by Jove!—Now you—Give us a sentence.

Æs. 'Tis rash and idle policy to foster
A lion's whelp within the city walls,
But when he's rear'd and grown you must indulge him.

Bac. By Jove then I'm quite puzzled; one of them
Has answer'd clearly, and the other sensibly:
But give us both of ye one more opinion;
—What means are left of safety for the state?

Eur. To tack Cinesias like a pair of wings
To Cleocritus' shoulders, and dispatch them
From a precipice to sail across the seas.

Bac. It seems a joke; but there's some sense in it.

Eur. . . . Then being both equipp'd with little cruets
They might co-operate in a naval action,
By sprinkling vinegar in the enemies' eyes.
—But I can tell you and will.

Bac.   Speak, and explain then—

Eur. If we mistrust where present trust is placed,
Trusting in what was heretofore mistrusted—

Bac. How! What? I'm at a loss—Speak it again
Not quite so learnedly—more plainly and simply.

Eur. If we withdraw the confidence we placed
In these our present statesmen, and transfer it
To those whom we mistrusted heretofore,
This seems I think our fairest chance for safety:
If with our present counsellors we fail,

Then with their opposites we might succeed.

Bac. That's capitally said, my Palamedes!
My politician! was it all your own?
Your own invention?

Eur.   All except the cruets;
That was a notion of Cephisophon's.

Bac. (to Æschylus). Now you—what say you?

Æs.   Inform me about the city—
What kind of persons has she placed in office?
Does she promote the worthiest?

Bac.   No, not she,
She can't abide 'em.

Æs.   Rogues then she prefers?

Bac. Not altogether, she makes use of 'em.
Perforce as it were.

Æs.   Then who can hope to save
A state so wayward and perverse, that finds
No sort of habit fitted for her wear?
Drugget or superfine, nothing will suit her!

Bac. Do think a little how she can be saved.

Æs. Not here; when I return there, I shall speak.

Bac. No, do pray send some good advice before you.

Æs. When they regard their lands as enemy's ground,
Their enemy's possessions as their own,
Their seamen and the fleet their only safeguard,
Their sole resource hardship and poverty,
And resolute endurance in distress—

Bac. That's well,—but juries eat up everything,
And we shall lose our supper if we stay.

Pluto. Decide then—

Bac.   You'll decide for your own selves,
I'll make a choice according to my fancy.

Eur. Remember, then, your oath to your poor friend;

And, as you swore and promised, rescue me.

Bac. "It was my tongue that swore"—I fix on Æschylus.

Eur. O wretch! what have you done?

Bac.　　　　　　　　Me? done?　What should I?
Voted for Æschylus to be sure—Why not?

Eur. And after such a villainous act, you dare
To view me face to face—Art not ashamed?

Bac. Why shame, in point of fact, is nothing real:
Shame is the apprehension of a vision
Reflected from the surface of opinion—
—The opinion of the public—they must judge.

Eur. O cruel!—Will you abandon me to death?

Bac. Why perhaps death is life, and life is death,
And victuals and drink an illusion of the senses;
For what is Death but an eternal sleep?
And does not Life consist in sleeping and eating?

Pluto. Now, Bacchus, you'll come here with us within.

Bac. (*a little startled and alarmed*).
What for?

Pluto.　　　　　　　To be received and entertain'd
With a feast before you go.

Bac.　　　　　　　　That's well imagined,
With all my heart—I've not the least objection.

CHORUS.

Happy is the man possessing
The superior holy blessing
Of a judgment and a taste
Accurate, refined and chaste;
As it plainly doth appear
In the scene presented here;
Where the noble worthy Bard
Meets with a deserved reward,

Suffer'd to depart in peace
Freely with a full release,
To revisit once again
His kindred and his countrymen—
    Hence moreover
    You discover,
That to sit with Socrates,
In a dream of learned ease;
Quibbling, counter-quibbling, prating,
Argufying and debating
With the metaphysic sect,
Daily sinking in neglect,
Growing careless, incorrect,
While the practice and the rules
Of the true poetic Schools
Are renounced or slighted wholly,
Is a madness and a folly.

PLUTO.

Go forth with good wishes and hearty good-will,
And salute the good people on Pallas's hill;
Let them hear and admire father Æschylus still
In his office of old which again he must fill:
—You must guide and direct them,
Instruct and correct them,
With a lesson in verse,
For you'll find them much worse;
Greater fools than before, and their folly much more.
And more numerous far than the blockheads of yore—
—And give Cleophon this,
And bid him not miss,

But be sure to attend
To the summons I send:
To Nicomachus too,
And the rest of the crew
That devise and invent
  New taxes and tribute,
Are summonses sent,
  Which you'll mind to distribute.
Bid them come to their graves,
Or, like runaway slaves,
If they linger and fail,
We shall drag them to jail;
Down here in the dark
With a brand and a mark.

Æs. I shall do as you say;
But the while I'm away,
Let the seat that I held
Be by Sophocles fill'd,
As deservedly reckon'd
My pupil and second
In learning and merit
And tragical spirit—
And take special care;
Keep that reprobate there
Far aloof from the Chair;
Let him never sit in it
An hour or a minute,
By chance or design
To profane what was mine.

Pluto. Bring forward the torches!—The Chorus shall wait
And attend on the Poet in triumph and state
With a thundering chaunt of majestical tone
To wish him farewell, with a tune of his own.

Chorus.

Now may the powers of the earth give a safe and speedy
    departure
To the Bard at his second birth, with a prosperous happy
    revival,
And may the city, fatigued with wars and long revolu-
    tion,
At length be brought to return to just and wise resolu-
    tions;
Long in peace to remain—Let restless Cleophon hasten
Far from amongst us here—since wars are his only diver-
    sion,
Thrace his native land will afford him wars in abundance.